ANTs

USING
ALTERNATIVE AND
NON-TRADITIONAL INVESTMENTS
TO ALLOCATE YOUR ASSETS IN
AN UNCERTAIN WORLD

DR. BOB FROEHLICH

WILEY

John Wiley & Sons, Inc.

Published by John Wiley & Sons, Inc., Hoboken, New Jersey.
Published simultaneously in Canada.

For general information on our other products and services or for technical support, please contact our Customer Care Department within the United States at (800) 762-2974, outside the United States at (317) 572-3993 or fax (317) 572-4002.

Wiley also publishes its books in a variety of electronic formats. Some content that appears in print may not be available in electronic books. For more information about Wiley products, visit our web site at www.wiley.com.

Library of Congress Cataloging-in-Publication Data:

Froehlich, Robert J., author.
    ANTs : Using Alternative and Non-Traditional Investments to Allocate Your Assets in an Uncertain World / Dr. Bob Froehlich.
        p.   cm
    Includes index.
    ISBN 978-0-470-94499-8 (cloth); ISBN 978-1-118-01972-6 (ebk);
    ISBN 978-1-118-01973-3 (ebk); ISBN 978-1-118-01974-0 (ebk);
        1. Investments.   2. Asset allocation.   3. Portfolio management.   I. Title.
    HG4521.F8134   2011
    332.6—dc22
                                                                        2010045661

Printed in the United States of America

10   9   8   7   6   5   4   3   2   1

To my wife
Cheryl Ann

For her infinite belief,
Her constant inspiration,
And her enduring love

Although our intellect always longs for clarity and certainty, our nature often finds uncertainty fascinating.
— Carl von Clausewitz, Prussian military strategist

Contents

Contents

Contents

Introduction

There is nothing more difficult to take in hand, more perilous to conduct or more uncertain in its success than to take the lead in the introduction of a new order of things.
—Niccolò Machiavelli

Having been in and around this industry for over 30 years now, it is amazing to me how most investors still derive their basic investment decisions on whether they think we are in a bull market or a bear market. If we are in a bull market, most investors want to overweight stocks; conversely if we are in bear market, investors want to overweight bonds. Here is why.

In the most basic of terms, a bull market is when the stock market is going up; that's why you want to overweight stocks, and a bear market is when the market is going down; that is why you want to overweight bonds by underweighting stocks. Bulls and bears were chosen by Wall Street to depict different markets by the way these animals kill their prey. A bull uses its horns and tosses its prey upward (hence we call an "up" market a bull market). A bear meanwhile uses its massive claws and slashes downward on its prey (hence we call a "down" market a bear market).

The problem with this simplified, outdated investment strategy is that it doesn't work anymore. Most investors are focusing on the wrong animals. It's no longer about bulls and bears; it's about insects. Instead of bulls and bears, we should be looking at butterflies and ANTs (alternative and non-traditional asset classes). This book introduces you to them, and shows you how they will be more meaningful to your portfolio than the traditional animal symbols.

The Butterfly Effect

In the early 1960s Edward Lorenz, a meteorologist, attempted to model the weather for the entire globe in a comprehensive computer program. This model was programmed with certain initial conditions based on accurate data and was then instructed to predict the weather. Finally, the initial conditions were very, very slightly altered in what would appear to be a very, very insignificant amount, especially from a global weather perspective; however, the results from these insignificant changes produced wildly dramatic impacts in weather patterns around the globe. The phenomenon became known as the "butterfly effect" because it was theorized that the simple movement of a butterfly's wings in the Amazon basin could change the wind current in South America, which could alter cloud formations over the Pacific Ocean, which would cause it to snow in Russia . . . all because a butterfly flapped its wings in the Amazon.

Introduction

The global trends that have been driving the stock markets and bond markets today can best be explained by this same butterfly effect. There are two very important lessons to be learned from the butterfly effect for the stock and bond markets. First, the entire world is connected by some fiber in some way. That means that all of the stock markets and bonds markets are also connected. There is no longer any corner of the earth in which you can hide in a stock market or a bond market. Second, something that may appear insignificant on the surface can set off a chain reaction that produces dramatic results.

This butterfly effect is more important to the stock market and bond market than it is to the weather. Stock market and bond market investors need to understand there is no longer any market anywhere that isn't connected. Markets may be connected from a direct or indirect economic perspective, or from a political or a social perspective, or even a psychological perspective. It doesn't matter what fiber connects the stock markets and bond markets; the fact remains that we are all interconnected. In this New World Order, globalization has turned previously isolated problems into everyone's problems. There is nowhere to hide.

Because all of the stock markets and bond markets are connected, the impact of what appears on the surface to be a somewhat minor isolated event, like Dubai World defaulting on its debt, or Thailand devaluing its currency, or Greece teetering toward financial collapse, may first be felt by countries in close proximity, but eventually it is felt around the globe in every single market, no matter how big or small. These unrelated events will even be felt in the world's largest stock market and bond market in the United States, despite the fact that these markets seemed to have nothing to do with Dubai World or Thailand or Greece.

Think of it this way: Every event around the globe will at some point in time impact every market; it may take a minute, an hour, a day, or even a year, but it will happen. Because all of the stock markets and bond markets are now interconnected, there is no longer such a thing as an irrelevant or isolated event. There was a time when investors in the U.S. stock market and U.S. bond market didn't need to worry about what was happening in China or Brazil or Poland or Indonesia. Not anymore! Everything that happens anywhere around the globe will eventually have an impact either positive or negative on all stock markets and bond markets.

Finally, don't forget the role technology and the media are playing. Because of the information superhighway and all of the media outlets, we find out about things faster, which makes stock markets and bond markets move even quicker, which makes them even more volatile.

The butterfly has made the bull and bear obsolete. Investors can no longer get the diversification they need by investing in different stock markets or bond markets around the world. They have to look at the world differently, meaning they have to look beyond just stocks and bonds into ANTs—alternative and non-traditional asset classes. I believe the butterfly effect is creating eight dominant alternative and non-traditional asset classes beyond just stocks and bonds. Eventually every investor will have some form of investment exposure to these asset classes.

In This Book

Chapter 1, "The 90 Percent Factor" explains why asset allocation matters. Roger Ibbotson, a Yale finance professor and chairman of Ibbotson Associates published a landmark study entitled "Does Asset Allocation Policy Explain 40, 90 or 100 Percent of Performance?" The study concluded that more than 90 percent of a portfolio's return was explained by its asset allocation. Most investors do not realize that the single most important investment decision they make is asset allocation. They spend so much time and are so focused on trying to pick the right individual stock or bond that they are forgetting that in the long run it's the asset allocation that matters the most, not the individual stock or bond you invest in.

The rest of the book is broken into two parts. Part One covers the eight asset classes:

Chapter 2, "If You Build It, They Will Come," explores commodities. All aspects of commodities are looked at, beginning with the energy-based commodities of oil and natural gas. Industrial-based commodities are next where I look at copper, steel, tin, and iron ore. Next up are precious metals where most of the attention is on gold and silver. Finally I look at possibly the most important group in commodities: agricultural or so-called soft commodities. These include corn, wheat, soybeans, cattle, and livestock.

Chapter 3, "Money Makes the World Go Round," explores the risk and opportunities of currency investing, as well as strategies that can be used. We look at currencies from two different perspectives, first from the developed markets like the United States, Japan, and Canada, then at the different risks and opportunities that emerging market currencies present in countries like China, India, and Brazil.

Chapter 4, "Get Real," focuses on the different economic cycles and opportunities that different real estate subclasses present. The primary focus is on the three real estate subclasses: residential, commercial, and industrial. The chapter concludes with a look at international real estate opportunities.

Chapter 5, "The Bridge to Everywhere," focuses on the foundation of every country's economy: roads, bridges, highways, airports, seaports, and anything that helps people or goods move faster and more efficiently. Within infrastructure, this chapter explores how the developed markets are more focused on improving and repairing their infrastructure while the emerging markets are more focused on creating and developing their infrastructure network. The chapter concludes by looking at the difference in investing in the companies that actually build the infrastructure as opposed to companies that are the operators of infrastructure after it has been built.

Chapter 6, "Follow the Bouncing Ball," makes the case for having exposure to investment products that will actually do better when interest rates are rising. These products are commonly referred to as floating rate products. Their rates float higher as interest rates move higher. Special focus is paid to a subasset class of senior secured floating rate bank loans, which present very unique investment opportunities to the retail investor.

Chapter 7, "Up, Up, and Away," looks at inflation hedges. In other words, make sure that your asset allocation includes some exposure to an asset class that is going to do better in a rising inflation environment. The best inflation hedge there is, in my opinion, is a product called Treasury Inflation Protected Securities or TIPS. This chapter shows you how they work and why you need them.

Chapter 8, "'Derivatives' Isn't a Dirty Word," reviews the three major classes of derivatives: futures and forwards (contracts to buy or sell an asset on or before a future date at a price specified today), options (another type of contract that gives the owner the right, but not the obligation, to buy or sell an asset), and swaps (contracts to exchange cash flows on or before a specified future date based on the underlying value of an asset). The chapter ends with a look at the five types of underlying derivatives: interest rate derivatives, foreign exchange derivatives, credit derivatives, equity derivatives, and commodity derivatives.

Chapter 9, "Garage Sale Anyone?" assesses the problems and unique opportunities associated with having collectibles as part of your asset allocation. The major collectibles this chapter focuses on rare art, rare coins, stamps, classic cars, and wine.

Part Two offers specific investing advice for ANTs:

Chapter 10, "ANTs Go Marching Two by Two," just might be the single most important chapter in the entire book. It explains that if you are going to invest in these alternative and non-traditional asset classes, do not do it alone. You need the help and assistance of a financial adviser. This chapter explains why, and then shows you how to choose one and what you should look for in a financial adviser.

Chapter 11, "The Axis of Evil," explores the three most common mistakes investors make after they have invested in alternative and non-traditional asset classes. I refer to these three mistakes as "the axis of evil." The first mistake is the desire to rebalance these assets too often. The second mistake is revising your plan for the wrong reason. The third mistake is to attempt to do it yourself. I put this third axis in for anyone who skipped over Chapter 10.

Chapter 12, "Ant Attack," puts everything together, so hopefully you can make some money investing in alternative investments. The highlight of this chapter is "Dr. Bob's ANTs Portfolio," complete with specific asset allocation targets and strategies ready to be implemented.

Each chapter ends with a box titled "ANT Valorem." (*Ad Valorem* is the Latin term meaning "according to value.") ANT Valorem is my new investment term that summarizes for you how to add value to your investments using ANTs.

The book also includes an Appendix, "ANTSpeak," a glossary that includes not only definitions for the terms in the book—but also my opinions regarding the importance, the significance, and the relevance of those terms. It is the first opinionated glossary of alternative and non-traditional asset investment terms. You won't want to miss it.

It's the Little Things

Remember that it's the little things in life that sometimes matter most, just as it's the little things in investing, like having exposure to ANTs (alternative and non-traditional assets), that just might be the most significant thing you can do. Come to think of it, there may not be many things smaller than an ANT. However, don't let that size fool you. Bill Vaughn, American columnist and author, put it best when he quipped, "Size isn't everything. The whale is endangered, while the ANT continues to do just fine."

Hopefully my ANTs will help you and your investments to do just fine as well.

CHAPTER ONE

The 90 Percent Factor

WHY ASSET ALLOCATION MATTERS

*Never walk away from failure. On the contrary, study it
carefully and imaginatively for its hidden assets.*
— Michael Korda, novelist

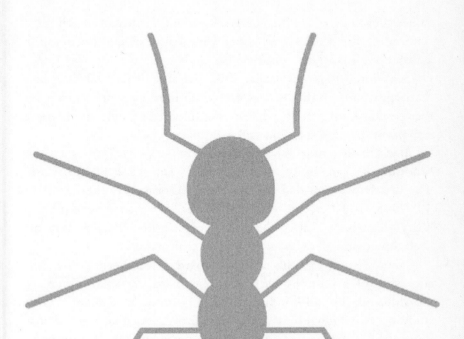

Before jumping into a discussion of how investors should be investing in alternative and non-traditional investment classes, first we need to understand how important it is to your investment return. In fact, in my view, the assets that you choose to invest in, which form the foundation for your personal asset allocation plan, are the single most important factor of all. It's not the underlying stock or bond that you spend so much time on that matters, but rather it is the amount you allocate to stocks, bonds, and alternative and non-traditional assets that will have the greatest impact on your investment results.

One Report (Ibbotson/Kaplan) . . .

Roger Ibbotson, a Yale finance professor and chairman of Ibbotson Associates, and Paul Kaplan, vice president and chief economist at Ibbotson Associates, published a landmark study on this topic. I am honored to know Roger Ibbotson and thrilled to have had the opportunity to discuss this issue with him, one on one. Maybe that is why I am convinced that asset allocation is the single most important decision that you will ever make.

Back to the study. The *Financial Analysts Journal* published the Ibbotson/Kaplan study in their 2001 January/February issue. The article was entitled, "Does Asset Allocation Policy Explain 40, 90 or 100 Percent of Performance?" This study gets to the heart of an issue that is clearly the most hotly debated issue on Wall Street, and all of Main Street, for that matter.

The question that this study addressed is whether it is the asset allocation of a portfolio or a portfolio manager's skill in picking individual stocks and bonds that drives portfolio performance. The study overwhelmingly concluded and proved once and for all that more than 90 percent of a portfolio's long-term return is explained by its asset allocation. Only a small portion of the return is explained by the manager's individual stock or bond selections.

> *The Ibbotson/Kaplan study overwhelmingly concluded and proved once and for all that more than 90 percent of a portfolio's long-term return is explained by its asset allocation.*

. . . After Another (Brinson, Hood, Beebower)

This Ibbotson/Kaplan report was an updated version of a study that had been done almost 20 years earlier. In 1986, Gary Brinson,

The 90 Percent Factor

L. Randolph Hood, and Gilbert Beebower analyzed the returns of 91 large U.S. pension plans between 1974 and 1983. The findings of their study were published in the July/August 1986 *Financial Analysts Journal.* The article was "Determinants of Portfolio Performance." Their study concluded that the single most significant portion of a portfolio's performance is asset allocation.

Brinson, Beebower, and Singer published a follow-up study in 1991. Their findings were again published in the *Financial Analysts Journal* in the May/June issue and called "Determinants of Portfolio Performance II: An Update." This follow-up confirmed the results of their first study and concluded that more than 90 percent of a portfolio's long-term return characteristics are determined by asset allocation.

There is clearly overwhelming evidence that a large percentage of a portfolio's performance is determined by the percentage of money that an investor places in stocks, bonds, and alternative and non-traditional assets. Then to a much lesser extent, the performance of a portfolio is affected by the individual's investment selection within those asset classes. The purpose of this book is to help you decide how much of that important 90 percent portion of your portfolio should be allocated to alternative and non-traditional asset classes.

When most individual investors thought of asset allocation, they simply thought of the big three: stocks, bonds, and cash. The reason was that most individual investors really only had these choices available to them. Not so anymore.

Individual investors now have the opportunity to invest just like the big institutional investors by having exposure to alternative and non-traditional asset classes as well.

It is still important for your portfolio to have traditional assets like stocks, bonds, and cash. Think of this allocation as a start instead of the finish. It is good, but it is really not good enough. Investing in alternative and non-traditional asset classes will help to protect your portfolio from downside harm and enhance its long-term performance.

The advantage of adding alternative and non-traditional assets to a portfolio is that they tend to exhibit low correlation with the traditional big three of stocks, bonds, and cash. It is for that reason, that including alternative and non-traditional asset classes in a portfolio has the potential to lower overall portfolio risk while increasing the long-term returns.

Think of it this way. Suppose you and I go to Las Vegas to play a new card game called investing. The dealer asks the first player, me, how many cards I want. I respond by saying I will take 11. One each for stocks, bonds, cash, commodities, currencies, real estate, infrastructure, interest rate hedges, inflation hedges, derivatives, and collectibles. The dealer then asks you how many cards you would like. You respond by saying you will take just three, representing stocks, bonds, and cash. Do you really think that you can beat me with that hand in the long run? If you are still investing by only using a few of the cards, there is no way you can win in the long run.

> *The advantage of adding alternative and non-traditional assets to a portfolio is that they tend to exhibit low correlation with the traditional big three of stocks, bonds, and cash.*

No Risk-Free Investments

Many investors shy away from alternative and non-traditional assets because they are still convinced that they can find risk-free investments by simply staying in the big three of stocks, bonds, and cash. Let me make this perfectly clear to you:

THERE IS NO SUCH THING AS A RISK-FREE INVESTMENT.

Currently the lowest-risk investment in the U.S. financial market is a U.S. Treasury bill. This is a government-guaranteed investment that matures in one year or less. In the world of Wall Street, these Treasury bills are commonly referred to as risk free. They are considered risk free because of their short maturity and government guarantee. In my opinion, "risk free" is a very inappropriate choice of terms. I would be the first to admit that Treasury bills provide a reliable positive return; however, that return can sometimes be more than offset by inflation and taxes. To me that is not risk free.

There have been several periods in time in which the rate of return on Treasury bills has not kept pace with inflation. That means that if short-term interest rates are below the inflation rates, investors in Treasury bills are losing purchasing power. That means that money invested in Treasury bills will buy fewer goods and services one year from today than it does now.

Taxes are also a big drag on investment return. Depending on an individual's federal income tax rate the return for Treasury bills could easily become negative. So how is that risk free? You invest in Treasury bills, and after you account for lost purchasing power due to inflation and after paying taxes on your investment return you are actually losing money with this so-called risk free investment.

Forget the Other 10 Percent

Let me end this chapter where I began. Why would you spend most of your time and most of your effort chasing something that may get you 10 percent of your goal? But that's exactly what most individual investors do as they spend massive amounts of effort to build a portfolio based on stock picking. Forget that 10 percent and instead focus on the 90 percent that really matters. As you focus on that 90 percent, the only question you have to answer is *Do I want to invest like a novice individual investor or like a sophisticated institutional investor?* If you are happy being a novice individual investor by investing only in stocks, bonds, and cash, you can stop reading now! If, however, you want to learn how to invest just like the sophisticated institutional investors by having exposure beyond just stocks, bonds, and cash to alternative and non-traditional asset classes like commodities, currencies, real estate, infrastructure, interest rate hedges, inflation hedges, derivatives, and collectibles, then hold on tight as we are about to explore the world of alternative and non-traditional asset classes.

My job on Wall Street is to forecast what is going to happen in the markets and the economy next week, next month, and next year. The fact of the matter is that no one really knows what will happen in the financial markets next week, next month, or next year, but we still have to invest for the future.

Having a broadly diversified asset allocation that includes exposure to alternative and non-traditional asset classes solves a problem that all investors face, how to manage investments without knowing the future. Asset allocation with a broad exposure to alternative and non-traditional assets eliminates the need to predict the future direction of the markets and eliminates the risk of being in the wrong market at the wrong time. Proper asset allocation does this by staying broadly diversified in assets that have a low correlation to one another. In other words, you want to have exposure to asset classes that don't move in tandem with the stock market and bond market.

It really is that simple. Focus on the 90 percent that truly matters, your asset allocation. When developing your asset allocation, make sure it is broadly diversified and has exposure to asset classes that have a low correlation to the stock market and bond markets; in other words, when the stock and bond markets zig you zag. If you follow those three steps of focusing on asset allocation, staying broadly diversified, and maintaining exposure to asset classes with a low correlation to the overall market—guess what—you will find yourself investing in alternative and non-traditional asset classes. I will be the first to admit that there are risks involved. But remember what I said earlier, there are no risk-free investments.

> *Asset allocation with a broad exposure to alternative and non-traditional assets eliminates the need to predict the future direction of the markets and eliminates the risk of being in the wrong market at the wrong time.*

In the chapters that follow, I show you how to identify the risks and find the opportunities of investing in alternative and non-traditional asset classes. Playwright Neil Simon gave us the best perspective of risk I have ever heard when he quipped, "If no one ever took risks, Michelangelo would have painted the Sistine floor."

 ANT Valorem

- More than 90 percent of a portfolio's long-term return characteristics are determined by asset allocation.
- Remember there have been several periods of time in which the rate of return on Treasury bills has not kept pace with inflation.
- When developing your asset allocation, make sure it is broadly diversified and has exposure to asset classes that have a low correlation to the stock market and bond market.
- Individual investors now have the opportunity to invest just like the big institutional investors do by having exposure to alternative and non-traditional asset classes—ANTs.

PART ONE

ANTs Come in a Variety of Shapes and Sizes

Eight ANT Asset Classes

CHAPTER TWO

If You Build It, They Will Come

INVESTING IN COMMODITIES

Gold still represents the ultimate form of payment in the world.
—Alan Greenspan

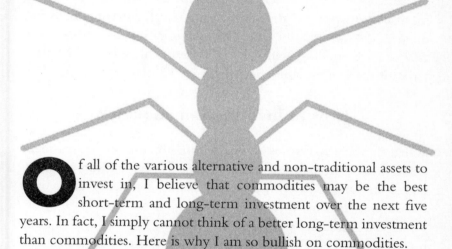

Of all of the various alternative and non-traditional assets to invest in, I believe that commodities may be the best short-term and long-term investment over the next five years. In fact, I simply cannot think of a better long-term investment than commodities. Here is why I am so bullish on commodities.

At the end of 2009, something happened that had never happened before in the entire history of mankind. Emerging market economies superseded the economies of the developed world. That's right; emerging market economies now represent the majority of the world's economies. So that we are all on the same page: When Wall Street refers to developed markets, they are talking about the United States, Japan, Germany, France, and countries like that. However, when Wall Street talks about emerging markets, I want you to think of China, India, Brazil, Poland, and Indonesia.

This fundamental economic shift is creating possibly the greatest demand ever witnessed for commodities. Here is one way to think about it from a commodity perspective. Think of developed markets as "improvers" while emerging markets are "builders."

Watch the impact this will have on commodity demand. Let me use infrastructure as a great example here. The developed world, like the United States and Japan, are improvers—as we add a turn lane or a new exit to our already existing infrastructure network and system. Meanwhile, emerging countries like China and Brazil are builders—and they are creating eight-lane highways. Now realize that the majority of the world's economy, the driving force over the next decade, will not simply be adding turn lanes; instead, they will be busy building eight-lane highways. This just might set the stage for the greatest commodity boom of all time.

How to Invest in Commodities

When thinking about how to invest in commodities you can head down one of two paths. Either get direct exposure to the underlying commodity itself or invest in companies that will benefit from this commodity's demand boom.

If you think the price of oil is heading higher, you want to have direct exposure to that commodity so you will benefit side by side and dollar for dollar as oil climbs. If oil is at $75 a barrel and you think it could go to $100 a barrel, you want direct exposure to oil. Conversely if oil is at $75 a barrel and you think the next stop is $50 a barrel, your better investment would be in oil-related stocks like ExxonMobil as it will not move down dollar for dollar. It would be the same with lumber. If you think the price is moving higher, you want direct exposure to that commodity. If, however, the price is headed lower, the better investment would be the stock of International Paper, again, because it won't fall dollar for dollar.

So what is the best way to invest in commodities? That is easy, both ways! If you have both direct exposure to these various commodities as well as an investment in the stocks that are closely associated with these commodities, you get the best of both worlds. You participate on the upside with your direct exposure to the commodity, and you protect yourself on the downside with your exposure to the stocks that are aligned with those commodities. The reason is if oil falls $2 a barrel in one day the stock of ExxonMobil doesn't fall dollar for dollar the same $2. This is what gives you your downside protection.

In this chapter I focus on all four of the major investment classifications of commodities: energy-based, industrial-based, precious metal-based, and agricultural-based.

If you have both direct exposure to these various commodities as well as an investment in the stocks that are closely associated with these commodities, you get the best of both worlds.

Energy Commodities: Fuel the World

One of the best reasons to think about why you should invest in energy commodities can be found in China. Beginning August 8, 2008, and ending August 24, 2008, China hosted the Olympics in Beijing. The theme was "One World One Dream." Before the Olympics, Beijing had five concentric circle beltways. They added four more to get them nine for the Olympics. No city (not New York, not London, or even Tokyo) in the world has two concentric circle beltways, and Beijing has nine of them. There were 15,000 different highway projects built in preparation for the Olympics.

This added 162,000 kilometers (or 100,000 miles) of new roads in China, enough to circle the earth four times at the equator.

Just think about the energy usage associated with all of this.

Oil

From an energy-based commodity perspective we focus on the big two—oil and natural gas—beginning with oil. It is only fitting to begin with oil as oil is the most actively traded of all commodities, and oil was the world's first trillion-dollar industry. While I can make the case that oil is the single most important commodity touching almost every aspect of our lives, it is scary how none of it is in our control. Publicly traded energy companies control a little over 10 percent of the world's oil reserves, and the rest is controlled by governments and their national oil companies.

In my mind, oil demand has nowhere to go but up. One has to look no further than China with its 1.3 billion people to figure out why. We are witnessing a transportation evolution rather than a revolution. Having visited China on numerous occasions, I have witnessed the mode of transportation evolving. It has moved from walking to bicycles, to public transportation to mopeds, and finally to automobiles. As the transportation evolution evolves, the demand for oil and gasoline will skyrocket.

While transportation may be an evolution, in the automotive industry in China it clearly is a revolution. Vehicle sales in China have now passed vehicle sales in the United States for the first time in history, and that is not all. China is also the world's largest manufacturer of vehicles. They did this despite the fact that they did not export one vehicle. That is about as bullish a sign as one could hope for regarding oil.

Natural Gas

Natural gas is a fossil fuel that is colorless, odorless, and emits few pollutants. The main component of natural gas is methane. Methane has a wide range of uses, from generating electricity to incineration. It is also widely used in the manufacturing of plastic, chemicals, and the pharmaceutical industry.

There are three ways to think about investing in the natural gas process: Companies that find it, drill for it, or distribute it. Where do you find it? That's easy—deep below the earth's surface. There are actually two different kinds of rock formations that could contain natural gas. What Wall Street refers to as *conventional natural gas* comes from wells where the gas tends to flow pretty freely from porous rocks and sandstone. *Unconventional natural gas* is packed tightly in rock formations like coal and shale, and you must break through these rocks to release the gas.

In the old days, geologists used to examine rock formations to find the energy reserves. That proved to be a hit or miss prospect. With all of the technology we have around us today, this process now involves seismic exploration. Seismic exploration actually involves shaking the ground and recording the waves that reflect off the rock formations to locate the natural gas. Companies like CGG Veritas specialize in gathering the seismic data.

After you have found the natural gas, you have to drill for it. A giant structure is set up above ground to allow for a hole to be dug deep into the earth. However, getting natural gas is not that simple. A tube is then inserted into the well (called casing) and it is filled with cement. Small explosives are then used to make holes in the casing and the surrounding rock formation. After that, water and air at extremely high pressure are pumped into the casing which further splits the rocks, freeing the natural gas and allowing it to flow into the casing of the well. This process is called "fracking," short for fracturing the rocks. You could invest in companies like Nabors Industries, which sets up, operates, and dismantles these wells. Or you could invest in companies like Halliburton, which provides products to companies like Nabors Industries to improve the drilling process.

So first we find the natural gas and drill for it. Then we have to distribute it. The biggest buyers of natural gas are oil companies and utilities. It is transferred to them using a vast network of pipelines. While some companies own pipelines, most companies simply pay to have access to other pipelines. You can even invest in a company like Spectra Energy that focuses almost solely on distribution by charging a pipeline toll to use their vast natural gas pipeline network.

Industrial Commodities: Build the World

Nowhere is there a better example of building the world than in Dubai. Business Bay (its central business district) will build 500 fifty-story skyscrapers. Dubai Waterfront, which is seven times the size of Manhattan, is a series of canals and islands. It added 500 miles of manmade waterfront property. Maybe the biggest story is in the area of land reclamation projects. The three Palm Islands in the shape of palm trees and World Archipelago, 300 individual islands in the shape of the world, make up the largest manmade reclamation project in the history of mankind. Just the fill material would equal a wall six-and-a-half feet high and two feet thick and would circle the earth three times at the equator. That was before they built anything at all; this was just the fill required to make the land.

They are building 100 high-end luxury hotels, 12,000 residence villas, and 10,000 shoreline apartment complexes, and that's not counting any of the individual homes, restaurants, parks, and theme parks. Just how big is it? It can be seen from outer space with the naked eye. Just think about all the industrial-based commodities that will be used.

Copper

Let's move on to the second major classification of commodities, those that are industrial-based. When the global economy is booming and people are buying cars and homes and appliances, the demand is first seen in industrial-based commodities like copper, aluminum, nickel, zinc, steel, tin, and iron ore.

Let's take a look at these industrial-based commodities, starting with copper. Maybe no commodity is a better indication of the health of the global economy than copper. The reason is that copper plays a big role in all construction, transportation, infrastructure, and telecommunications.

Let's look at one tiny piece of the global economy, residential housing. As the emerging market economies around the world strive to create a middle class, there will no doubt be a housing boom. What does that mean for copper? That means more copper demand for wiring for electricity, more copper demand for plumbing, and more copper demand for basic electrical appliances, all of which have huge amounts of copper inside. I think that you get the picture regarding copper demand.

What about supply? There have been no major discoveries of copper. Add that to the fact that most open-pit copper mines will run dry in the next decade, and you couldn't ask for a more bullish supply story to invest in. Not only that, when new discoveries are made, it takes time and a great deal of money to bring them into production.

Here is the bottom line. Inventories (supply) are low and demand, especially from booming emerging markets, is soaring. Add it all up, and there is not enough copper production to meet the demand for copper worldwide. One way to invest would be in copper mining companies like Rio Tinto or BHP Billiton. Or you can invest directly in copper through iPath Dow Jones-UBS Copper Subindex Total Return, which is structured to move dollar for dollar with the under-lying price of copper.

> *Maybe no commodity is a better indication of the*
> *health of the global economy than copper.*

Aluminum

Let's move on to aluminum. This is a metal that you see and touch every day, and you just don't think about it. Aluminum is one of the most widely used metals in the world. First, think planes, trains, and automobiles. Oh, and don't forget ships and trucks as well. It is also used for cookware, cans, and cooking foil. Don't forget alumi-num doors, window frames, and aluminum siding for houses. Did I mention transmission lines for electricity along with the production of paints? Don't forget a few of the old standbys: magnets, swords, and knives. Add to that the fact that aluminum is being used more and more in the automotive industry because it is lightweight and very friendly to use during the manufacturing process.

A very simple way to invest in aluminum would be in Alcoa. It is the third-largest aluminum producer in the world. Another way would be in Aluminum Corporation of China. It is involved in both the production and marketing of aluminum in China.

Nickel

Next stop along the metal spectrum is nickel. Nickel is often over-looked by investors because they fail to look beyond nickel to the number of by-products that use nickel and are in great demand. These include other metals like silver, platinum, cobalt, and palladium.

Nickel is primarily used as a refined metal with two-thirds of its usage for stainless steel. You can still find nickel in everyday things around you in addition to stainless steel, like chrome, coins, and pots and pans.

Nickel is now being used more for various military and aerospace uses. The reason these industries love nickel is because it is corrosion-resistant. The largest consumer of nickel in the world is China.

Around the globe the top producing countries are Canada, Russia, Australia, Indonesia, and Brazil. One way to invest in nickel is a Canadian company called Vale. It is a 100-year-old company that operates on four continents.

Zinc

One of the oldest commodities, zinc, can be traced all the way back to 1300 B.C., when it was used to make brass. Today, half of all zinc is used to galvanize steel to protect it from corrosion. About 20 percent is used to produce brass. Another 20 percent goes into the production of zinc-based alloys to supply the die casting industry. The remainder is used for compounds such as zinc oxide and zinc sulfate.

Zinc can be converted into a broad range of products that can be found in construction, transportation, consumer goods, electronics, and appliances.

The fastest-growing demand for zinc is in batteries. Zinc-based energy systems have tremendous advantages including recyclability, safety, and zero emissions. Zinc is used to manufacture a variety of batteries, both primary and rechargeable, for both consumer and industrial uses.

Add to that, battery usage worldwide is soaring. Why? Think demand for batteries in cell phones, cars, laptop computers, iPads, iPhones, and iEverything else. Zinc has played an increasingly large role in battery manufacturing as zinc-nickel, silver-zinc, and zinc-air batteries are replacing competing battery types such as lithium-ion. The reason is quite simple. Zinc-based batteries are less volatile, nontoxic and recyclable, and can hold more energy than similarly sized lithium-ion batteries. As battery usage continues to soar around the globe, at the same time that concerns over disposal of toxic used battery acids from lithium-ion batteries mount, the only answer is zinc.

One way to invest in zinc is through a Canadian company called Excalibur Resources, Ltd.

Steel

Since I was born and raised in the steel city of Pittsburgh, steel is my favorite of all commodities.

For any of you not from the steel city, steel is simply iron ore with carbon as a hardening agent. I should know as I worked four summers at U.S. Steel in Pittsburgh to pay my way through college.

What I really like about steel is that you are really not investing in steel, but rather in all of the other industries that need steel. Here are my top 10 industries that must have steel: infrastructure construction, commercial construction, both oil and gas exploration as well as oil and gas distribution, the automotive industry, appliances, water projects, wastewater projects, agriculture, and finally the aerospace industry.

If you think about it, there is not just one aspect of our economy that creates the demand for steel. Instead the demand for steel comes from a wide range of industries all across the globe.

How could you invest in steel? Well, you could use the Steel ETF (exchange-traded fund). The Steel ETF replicates the price and performance of the NYSE (New York Stock Exchange) Arca Steel

Index. That index is a modified market capitalization-weighted index comprised of publicly traded companies involved in the production of steel products or the mining or processing of iron ore. Or you could invest directly in one of those companies who are in the Steel ETF. United States Steel is typically a top 10 holding.

Tin

Once again this commodity, tin, goes back to about 3000 B.C., when its primary use was as an alloy with copper to make bronze. Today we mainly use it because of its resistance to corrosion as well as its use for electronic soldering as well as the most obvious use, food containers like tin cans.

Demand for tin has been steadily rising around the globe, while supply has been in a free fall. Indonesia is the world's largest producer of tin accounting for a little over one-third of the over-all global tin market. Exports from Indonesia are dropping for two reasons. First, Indonesia is nearing the end of its easily mined and high grade reserves. Everyone goes for the low hanging fruit first. Second, the government of Indonesia is cracking down on illegal mining. Most small and medium-sized tin smelters in Indonesia depend on supplies from somewhat crude family-owned mines. Since the government crackdown, many of these tin smelters have had to either greatly reduce tin output or shut down altogether due to lack of suppliers.

In addition, tin production in the third-largest exporter, Peru, is also falling. The stage is being set for a longer-term supply/demand imbalance, which should be bullish for tin in the long run. With this broad supply/demand fundamental imbalance perhaps the best way to invest is the broadest way, something like Barclay's iPath Dow Jones–UBS Tin Subindex Total Return. This product reflects the potential returns on tin futures contracts.

Iron Ore

When someone says iron ore, think steel. That's because 98 percent of iron ore is used to make steel, and as you know steel is one of my favorite commodities. While there are other uses for iron ore, it is not the amount but rather the ingenuity of how it can be used. Powdered iron ore is used in metallurgy products, magnets, and auto parts, while radioactive iron ore is used in medicine and in biochemical research. Finally blue iron ore is used in paints, printing inks, plastics, paper dyeing, and even cosmetics (eye shadow).

If you believe as I do that steel will continue to be in demand, then so too will the demand for iron ore. The world's largest producing nations are Australia, Brazil, China, India, Russia, and the United States.

There is no pure investment play for iron ore, so investors can choose one of two paths. They can invest in the above-mentioned Steel ETF, or they could invest in the stock of the three largest iron ore producers in the world: BHP Billiton, Rio Tinto, or Vale.

Precious Metal Commodities: Bling around the World

It's official: Emerging market economies (think China and Brazil, for example) have just surpassed the developed economies (think the United States and Japan). That's right; these emerging market economies now represent a majority of the global economy, accounting for over 50 percent. We need to come up with a new name, as they are no longer emerging; they have emerged. People in these emerging markets love to buy expensive things, and they especially love to wear and show their wealth. That is a very bullish sign for precious metals.

Silver

Let's now move on to the third major classification of commodities: precious metals. In this section I focus on the big three: silver, platinum/palladium, and gold, beginning with silver.

For over 4,000 years silver was regarded as a form of money. With the end of the silver standard, silver lost its role as legal tender in the United States. It was used in dimes and quarters until 1964 and in half dollars until 1970.

With countries like the United States no longer needing silver reserves to use silver as coinage, governments became net sellers. This caused a collapse in the demand for silver from governments; however, industrial manufacturers were on a buying frenzy. Why? The answer is quite simple. Silver is the most electrically conductive, thermally conductive, and reflective commodity in the world.

While we never think about it like this, modern life as we know it would not be possible without silver. Think photography, batteries, and electronics—all the things that came of age as World War II came to an end and the baby boomer generation was created. Add to that the scientific discoveries in the 1960s regarding the manufacturing and industrial uses of silver and it is easy to see why silver demand has exploded.

Let me give you a real quick frame of reference here between silver and gold. Gold has two basic uses: jewelry and money. Both of these uses are a form of hoarding as the gold doesn't get used up. In fact less than 10 percent of gold production is actually used in industrial applications. That means that 90 percent of all the gold ever mined throughout the history of the world is still available for purchase somewhere.

On the other hand, silver has hundreds of industrial uses and applications. Silver is used in batteries, biocides, brazing, electrical conductors, electroplating, jewelry, medical applications, mirrors, reflective coatings, photography, silverware, solar energy cells, and water purification. Of all of the above mentioned uses for silver, only jewelry and silverware result in saving the silver (hoarding it if you will) while in every other use silver will be used up in microscopic amounts that will be eventually thrown away.

You might be thinking, well if there is so much demand for silver, wouldn't they just mine more silver to meet that demand? The answer is not that simple. A majority of silver does not come from silver mines. Instead, silver is often a by-product of mining copper, lead, zinc, and gold. Over 75 percent of the supply of silver originates as a by-product of mining other metals.

As for getting investment exposure to silver, you can get it one of three ways. First you can invest directly in one of the world's leading silver miners, Coeur d'Alene Mining Corporation, in Coeur d'Alene, Idaho. The company has five producing silver mines in four countries.

Another way to invest in silver is in a company called Silver Wheaton. They may be one of the best pure silver plays, although they actually don't mine any silver. Instead they make all of their money through contracts to purchase by-product silver from other companies' mining operations. That way they obtain the silver at low fixed costs yet are still able to sell the silver at market prices. The company has only five employees with net sales approaching $300 million. Or you could invest in iShares Silver Trust, which invests exclusively in physical silver.

Platinum/Palladium

The precious metals platinum and palladium are found together in the same ores and both have similar but not identical characteristics. Palladium, for instance is less effective than platinum in most antipollution devices, especially those used with diesel engines.

Palladium is half the weight of platinum, so any jewelry made from it is much lighter.

While jewelry manufacturing provides most of the annual demand for gold, it is far less important for platinum and palladium where it accounts for less than 20 percent.

Most of the world's platinum comes from South Africa. South Africa is also the second-biggest producer of palladium, but palladium mostly comes as a by-product of nickel mining in Russia and Canada.

These precious metals get their real demand from the automatic catalytic devices now fitted to all new motor vehicles produced in developed countries. These catalytic devices referred to as catalytic converters actually convert poisonous exhaust gases such as oxides of nitrogen into water and other harmless substances in order to prevent air pollution. These catalytic converters account for over half the world's demand for platinum and palladium.

The remainder of the demand comes from a variety of industries. For example, these two precious metals are also used as catalysts in oil refining and chemical industries. They are also used in the manufacturing of a wide diversity of products such as computer monitors, mobile phones, hard disc drives, and electronic weaponry.

One way to invest would be with a company called Anglo Platinum, which is the world's largest producer of platinum and is a South African–based company. You could invest in an exchange-traded fund like ETFS Physical Platinum Shares ETF, which is designed to offer investors a return equivalent to the movement in the spot price of platinum.

Gold

Last but certainly not least, let's move on to the final and most important of all the precious metals, gold. This is because of all of the precious metals gold is the most popular as an investment. The reason is that most investors will buy gold as a safe haven against any political, social, or economic crisis. Investors also rush to gold if there are major stock market declines, or their country's national debt is skyrocketing, or there is high inflation, or the prospect of war is on the horizon.

I believe every investor should have some exposure to gold as an investment. To me there are numerous and compelling reasons to buy gold. First, central banks in several countries led by India and Saudi Arabia have begun to increase their gold holding as a form of currency reserve. Second, the worldwide production of gold is not keeping up with consumption. This out-of-balance demand will tend to push prices higher. Third, most gold consumption is done in India and China, and their demand is increasing with their increase in national wealth. Now instead of gold ownership being largely confined to jewelry, these countries are now easing barriers against investing directly in gold bullion.

There are a couple of ways to invest in gold. You could own the stock of two of the largest producers of gold in the world, Newmont Mining or Barrick Gold. You could invest in an exchange-traded fund like SPDR Gold Trust, whose objective is for the shares of the trust to reflect the price of gold bullion.

Agricultural Commodities: Feed the World

The final classification of commodities just might hold the greatest long-term potential of all: the agricultural-based commodities.

From a global perspective, every single day 275,000 people enter the middle class. That's like creating a new city the size of Venice, Italy, every single day of the year. Domestically speaking, it would be akin to creating a city the same size as Newark, New Jersey, or Anchorage, Alaska, every single day.

At the end of the year, that means we would have added 100 million people to the middle class. That would be the same as discovering a country like the Philippines or Mexico every single year, both with populations right around 100 million. The bulk of this middle class explosion will be in seven countries: Indonesia, China, India, Brazil, Mexico, Russia, and Turkey. As people move into the middle class their higher standard of wealth provides them with the ability to spend more on food and food-related products.

That is not even the most dramatic demographic shift to feed the world. Over the next decade over 2 billion people around the world will move from below the poverty level to above the poverty level. It is quite simple to predict exactly which behavior will change first when someone moves from below the poverty level to above the poverty level.

From a global perspective, every single day 275,000 people enter the middle class. That's like creating a new city the size of Venice, Italy, every single day of the year.

Maybe I should explain this by telling you what is not going to change first. They are not going to dramatically change their mode of transportation. They are still content walking, riding a bicycle, or using public transportation. The very first behavior that changes is not to run out and buy a new car.

They also don't immediately decide that now is the time to travel and take the family on vacation to Disney World. That is not what happens first. Here is what does. The very first behavior they change is the quality and quantity of the food they eat. After years of living below the poverty line, they are sick and tired of eating only beans, rice, or tortillas. They now want the good stuff. They want some protein. They want some meat, fish, and eggs added to their diet. When 2 billion people decide to eat more, I am not sure you could ask for a more bullish sign regarding the positive long-term direction for agricultural-based commodities.

Corn

Let's touch on a few of these agricultural-based commodities beginning with corn. Corn has been cultivated for thousands of years, originally domesticated by cultures in Central America. It eventually spread across the globe after Europeans had arrived in the New World.

Obviously, corn is most frequently used as a food source, both for human consumption (can you say corn on the cob?) and as feed for livestock. Corn can also be processed into many different products including cornmeal and corn syrup and the latest craze, biofuel in the form of ethanol.

Corn is quite fascinating from an investment perspective because there are numerous ways to invest in corn. Obviously you could invest in an exchange-traded fund like ETES Corn ETF, which trades on the London Stock Exchange. This fund is designed to track the Dow Jones–UBS Corn Subindex, which is composed of exchange-traded commodity futures contracts rather than physical commodities and reflects the return of a rolling, fully collateralized investment in corn commodity futures.

Or you could invest in a company whose profits are tied to corn consumption. The best fit here is a company called Archer Daniels Midland. Another way to invest in corn is to invest in farm equipment manufacturers. Corn has become a very capital-intensive product that now requires large-scale farm equipment for cultivation and harvesting. Companies such as John Deere and Caterpillar offer such an indirect way to invest in corn through heavy farm equipment.

Finally, because corn is used as a biofuel as a source for ethanol you could invest in a petroleum company that produces ethanol.

One such company is Chevron, which is the largest retail producer of ethanol.

Wheat

Let's now move on from corn to wheat. Maybe people don't realize it, but wheat is actually a grass. It is the third most produced cereal after maize and rice. Globally wheat is the leading source of vegetable protein as it has more protein than corn or rice.

Wheat grain is a staple food used to make flour and is used in breads, biscuits, cookies, cakes, cereal, paste, noodles, and my most favorite use for the fermentation to make beer.

Wheat is a little more difficult to invest in directly. There is no wheat exchange-traded fund. You could get some exposure through PowerShares DB Agriculture Fund, which is an exchange-traded fund that in addition to wheat also invests in corn, rice, soybeans, and sugar. This ETF actually holds futures contracts on the underlying commodities. Few if any bakeries are publicly traded, and none are a pure wheat play. Maybe the best wheat stock play would be cereal giant Kellogg. Or a company like Bunge that sells fertilizer to wheat farmers.

Sugar

Sugar just may hold the answer to countries who want to cut their reliance on petroleum and natural gas. The great thing about sugar cane as an energy source is that it is incredibly efficient. Many ethanol feed stocks, such as corn that I talked about earlier, require as much energy to grow and refine as they actually produce in energy. However, sugar cane production actually results in an unbelievable net positive energy gain. It has more than an eight to one ratio of energy output to energy input. That is especially so when it is grown in the country in which it is used, so there is no energy or cost expended on any transportation.

Now think about this: The more sugar cane that goes into fuel tanks the less there is for sweetening in candies, cookies, and soda. So the trend is clear; we will continue to consume more sugar than we can produce.

Here are two thoughts about how to invest in sugar. There is an exchange-traded fund called SGG-iPath Dow Jones–UBS Sugar Total Return Subindex. It is a single commodity index consisting of futures contracts on the commodity of sugar. Or you could invest in a company like Imperial Sugar that processes and markets refined sugar out of mills in Georgia and Louisiana under Imperial Sugar, Dixie Crystals, and Holly Sugar brands. Sounds like a sweet investment to me!

 ANT Valorem

- Remember, to invest in commodities you can head down two paths. You can either get direct exposure to the underlying commodity itself or invest in companies that will benefit from this commodity demand boom.
- Invest in copper directly through iPath Dow Jones–UBS Copper Subindex Total Return.
- Get your direct exposure to tin through Barclays iPath Dow Jones–UBS Tin Subindex Total Return.
- Of all of the precious metals, gold is the most popular. A great investment idea is an exchange-traded fund like SPDR Gold Trust.
- Corn can be directly invested through an exchange-traded fund, Dow Jones–UBS Corn Subindex.

CHAPTER THREE

Money Makes the World Go Round

How to Trade Currencies

The first panacea for a mismanaged nation is inflation of the currency; the second is war. Both bring a temporary prosperity; both bring a permanent ruin. But both are the refuge of political and economic opportunists.

—Ernest Hemingway

The currency market is also referred to as the foreign exchange market. On Wall Street we simply call it the forex market, or the FX market for short. It is the largest and most liquid of all the financial markets, and it is basically open around the clock six days a week.

The market is so big that even if someone is making a billion dollar trade and it is executed on the spot, it may not move currency prices all that much. Any other market in the world would either soar or collapse if someone bought or sold a billion dollars. The reason the currency market is so big is that every cross-border transaction must pass through the currency market at some stage. It could be a Chinese company buying a U.S. tool and die company, or the Singapore Pension fund deciding to invest in U.S. Treasury bonds, or a Brazilian company buying a German facility.

Again, every single cross-border transaction must at some time pass through the currency markets.

Let me try to put the size of the currency market into some perspective for you. The average daily currency trading volume is over $2 trillion a day; $2 trillion a day in trading is more than 10 times the daily trading volume of all of the world's stock markets combined. It is mind-boggling to try to put $2 trillion dollars into some perspective, but maybe this will help. If I gave you one second for every dollar that added up to $2 trillion or I gave you two trillion seconds, how long an amount of time do you think you would have? One hundred years, 1,000 years, or 10,000 years? None of the above. Try 64,000 years! Two trillion seconds of time is 64,000 years! Let's just leave it there and say the currency market is really BIG!

What Is Currency Trading?

The single most difficult issue for most investors to understand about currencies is that every single investment has two separate parts to it: You are buying and selling at the exact same trade. That means that every currency investment consists of a purchase and a sale.

Think about how easy the stock market and bond market are compared to the currency markets. When you buy a stock, let's say you buy 100 shares of Hartford, all you want to have happen is the price of Hartford stock to go up. Then you simply sell your 100 shares, and you have made money.

That is not the way the currency markets work. Remember the currency markets are also called the foreign exchange market. Think about just that "exchange" aspect for a moment. In currency investing the purchase of one currency involves the simultaneous sale of another currency. If you want to invest in the U.S.

dollar, you want it to go higher; however, it has to go higher against another currency. So in currency investing, if the dollar goes higher against another currency, that other currency has to also go lower against the dollar.

Let's go back to my Hartford stock purchase example to explain this exchange concept. In exchange terms in the stock market, when you buy Hartford stock you are selling cash, and conversely when you are selling your Hartford stock you are buying cash.

> *In currency investing, the purchase of one currency involves the simultaneous sale of another currency.*

It All Starts with the U.S. Dollar

The U.S. dollar is the central currency against which all other currencies are traded. In fact the U.S. dollar is on one side or another of 90 percent of all currency market transactions. Why? First, the United States is the largest economy in the entire world. Second, the United States has the largest and most liquid financial markets in the world. Third, because all commodities are priced in U.S. dollars, most cross-border transactions involve the U.S. dollar if they involve commodities. Think of it this way: Even if you are an oil importer from Argentina buying crude oil from Oman, you are still going to have to pay in U.S. dollars.

Currency investments can actually be classified into three groups:

1. Major pairs
2. Minor pairs
3. Cross pairs

Each is covered in more detail next.

Major Pairs

There are three major currency pairs or currency trades or investments:

1. Euro-dollar (EUR/USD)
2. Dollar-yen (USD/JPY)
3. Sterling-dollar (GBP/USD)

First, is the euro-dollar, where you are focused on the countries of the United States and the European countries that comprise the eurozone. The two currencies involved are the dollar (USD) and the euro (EUR). The second major pair is the dollar-yen, where you are focused on the countries of the United States and Japan. The two currencies involved are the dollar (USD) and the yen (JPY). The third major pair is the sterling-dollar, where you are focused on the countries of the United States and the United Kingdom. The two currencies involved are the dollar (USD) and the British pound sterling (GBP).

Minor Pairs

There are four minor currency trades or investments:

1. Dollar-swissy (USD/CHF)
2. Dollar-loonie (USD/CAD)
3. Aussie-dollar (AUD/USD)
4. Kiwi-dollar (NZD/USD)

Again all of these involve the U.S. dollar. The first is the dollar-swissy, where you are focused on the countries of the United States and Switzerland. The two currencies involved are the dollar (USD) and the Swiss franc (CHF). Second is the dollar-loonie, where you are focused on the countries of the United States and Canada.

The two currencies involved are the dollar (USD) and the Canadian dollar (CAD), which is also called the loon. The third is the aussie-dollar where you are focused on the countries of the United States and Australia. The two currencies involved are the dollar (USD) and the Australian dollar (AUD). The fourth and final minor pair is the kiwi-dollar, where you are focused on the countries of New Zealand and the United States. The two currencies involved are the New Zealand dollar (NZD) and the dollar (USD).

Cross Pairs

A cross-currency pair is any currency pair that does not include the U.S. dollar. The three most actively traded crosses focus on the three major non–U.S. dollar currencies of Europe, Japan, and the United Kingdom, and are referred to on Wall Street as euro crosses, yen crosses, and sterling crosses.

There are five euro crosses:

1. Euro-swissy (EUR/CHF)
2. Euro-sterling (EUR/GBP)
3. Euro-loonie (EUR/CAD)
4. Euro-aussie (EUR/AUD)
5. Euro-kiwi (EUR/NZD)

First is the euro-swissy, where you are focused on the countries comprising the eurozone and Switzerland. The two currencies involved are the euro (EUR) and the Swiss franc (CHF). The second euro cross is the euro-sterling, where you are focused on the countries that comprise the eurozone and the United Kingdom. The two currencies involved are the euro (EUR) and the British pound sterling (GBP). The third euro cross is the euro-loonie, where you are focused on the countries that comprise the eurozone and Canada. The two currencies involved are the euro (EUR) and the Canadian dollar (CAD). The fourth euro cross is the euro-aussie, where you are focused on the countries that comprise the eurozone and Australia. The two currencies involved are the euro (EUR) and the Australian dollar (AUD). The fifth and final euro cross is the euro-kiwi, where you are focused on the countries that comprise the eurozone and New Zealand. The two currencies involved are the euro (EUR) and the New Zealand dollar (NZD).

There are six yen crosses:

1. Euro-yen (EUR/JPY)
2. Sterling-yen (GBP/JPY)
3. Swissy-yen (CHF/JPY)
4. Aussie-yen (AUD/JPY)
5. Kiwi-yen (NZD/JPY)
6. Loonie-yen (CAD/JPY)

The first is the euro-yen, where you are focused on the countries that comprise the eurozone and Japan. The two currencies involved are the euro (EUR) and the Japanese yen (JPY). The second yen cross is called the sterling-yen, where you are focused on the United Kingdom and Japan. The two currencies are the British pound sterling (GBP) and the Japanese yen (JPY). The third yen cross is the swissy-yen, where you are focused on the countries of Switzerland and Japan. The two currencies are the Swiss franc (CHF) and the Japanese yen (JPY). The fourth yen cross is the aussie-yen, where you are focused on the countries of Australia and Japan. The two currencies are the Australian dollar (AUD) and the Japanese yen (JPY). The fifth yen cross is the kiwi-yen, where you are focused on the countries of New Zealand and Japan. The two currencies are the New Zealand dollar (NZD) and the Japanese yen (JPY). The sixth and final yen cross is the loonie-yen, where you are focused on the countries of Canada and Japan. The two currencies are the Canadian dollar (CAD) and the Japanese yen (JPY).

There are only four sterling crosses:

1. Sterling-swissy (GBP/CHF)
2. Sterling-loonie (GBP/CAD)
3. Sterling-aussie (GBP/AUD)
4. Sterling-kiwi (GBP/NZD)

The first is the sterling–swissy, where you are focused on the countries of the United Kingdom and Switzerland. The two currencies involved are the British pound sterling (GBP) and the Swiss franc (CHF). The second is the sterling-loonie, where you are focused on the countries of the United Kingdom and Canada. The two currencies involved are the British pound sterling (GBP) and the Canadian dollar (CAD). The third sterling cross is the sterling-aussie, where you are focused on the countries of the United Kingdom and Australia. The two currencies involved are the British pound sterling (GBP) and the Australian dollar (AUD). The fourth and final sterling cross is the sterling-kiwi, where you are focused on the countries of the United Kingdom and New Zealand. The two currencies involved are the British pound sterling (GBP) and the New Zealand dollar (NZD).

How to Invest in Currencies

Now that you have a solid idea of what you can actually invest in, the remainder of this chapter focuses on what to look for and how to invest in currencies. I don't want to oversimplify, but the single most important thing to focus on as a currency investor is interest rates.

As equity investors, the only thing that really matters is earnings. If a company has strong earnings, eventually that company's stock is going high. Conversely, if that same company has no earnings, that company's stock is headed lower. For a currency investor, the same is true with interest rates. If interest rates are heading higher, that currency will get stronger; if interest rates are going lower, that currency is getting weaker.

Interest rates for the most part are controlled by the central bank that determines a country's monetary policy (whether it raises or lowers rates). Interest is a very important fact influencing overall economic activity and strength. Lower interest rates typically stimulate borrowing, investment, and consumption, while higher interest rates decrease borrowing and decrease consumption.

Interest rates are critical for currencies because they drive the ultimate direction of the global flow of all capital. That is because interest rates serve as the objective reference for what investors should expect to earn in any given country. Think of it this way, would you rather have an investment that yields 5 percent or 2 percent? Obviously you want the higher-yielding 5 percent investment. That's exactly the same with currencies. Currencies with higher yields, meaning higher interest rates, go up, while currencies with lower yields, meaning lower interest rates go down.

> *If interest rates are heading higher, that currency will get stronger; if interest rates are going lower, that currency is getting weaker.*

Interest Rate Expectations

One of the things that make currency investing so challenging and so exciting is that it is not as simple as what the current interest rate levels are. The currency markets are actually more focused on what the future direction of interest rates are going to be—higher or lower? The reason this is so important is because the current interest rate levels are already reflected in the currency's value. So think what that could mean for a currency investor. It's not enough to invest in a currency because that country currently has high interest rates. If the markets expect interest in that country to move lower in the future, that country's currency is likely headed lower right now. The same is true on the other side of the coin. You can't avoid the currencies from countries with low interest rates because if the markets expect interest rates to go higher, they will drive up the value of that country's currency today.

Clearly the most challenging aspect of currency investing is how dramatically expectations change completely. Unlike the equity markets where expectations may change regarding how much a company is going to earn or lose, it never shifts for an all-time record in earnings to the lowest loss in the entire history of the company. In currency markets drastic shifts are common. The currency market unlike maybe any other market tends to overreact to every single data point. For example, market expectations may be for an interest rate cut; however, in one day the economic releases show a much lower unemployment rate, meaning a stronger employment market along with a surprise uptick in the Consumer Price Index. At that point market expectations now expect the next move to be a rate increase, and the currency has a big rally all because of one day's worth of economic releases. Currencies can go from big losers to big winners back to big losers again all driven by the weekly economic releases.

Everything Is Relative

As a currency investor remember that even if you have a good idea of what a country's interest policy is going to be, that still doesn't tell you all you need to know about whether a currency is headed higher or lower. As a currency investor, don't get overly focused on one country's interest rates. Remember it's one country's interest rates in relation to another country's interest rates that matter.

Remember, in currency investing you must focus on currency pairs, meaning one country's currency value relative to another country's currency value. On Wall Street we call the difference between the two interest rates of the two currencies the "interest rate differential." This interest rate differential is the single most important spread for currency investors to watch. If you find an increasing interest rate differential, that will always be good for the higher-yielding currency. Conversely, anytime you spot a narrowing interest rate differential that always favors the lower-yielding currency.

The biggest moves in the currency markets always occur when two countries' monetary policies (interest rates) are headed or, I should say, are thought to be headed in opposite directions—one going higher and the other lower or vice versa. It's a little like doubling down. If you focus on the interest rate differential, you can see that when rates are heading in the opposite direction, one-half these changes get amplified, which is just like doubling down. Think about it this way; instead of one country's currency depreciating based on an expected ¼ percent interest rate cut, the second currency appreciates based on an expected ½ percent rate hike. So now you are looking at a ¾ percent interest rate differential and not just a ¾ percent.

> *The biggest moves in the currency markets always occur when two countries' monetary policies (interest rates) are headed or, I should say, are thought to be headed in opposite directions—one going higher and the other lower or vice versa.*

Real Rates Matter Most

As a currency investor, you can't simply focus on nominal interest rates, the actual printed interest rate you see. It is much more important to focus on real interest rates. Real interest rates are actually the inflation-adjusted rates, which are the above-mentioned nominal interest rates minus the Consumer Price Index, which is the proxy for inflation. It is easier to use a bond investment as an example. So even if a bond carries a nominal of 9.0 percent, if the annual rate of inflation in the country is 6.5 percent, the real yield on the bond is closer to 2.5 percent.

This is especially true in these upstart emerging markets. Let's say that nominal interest rates are 17 percent. If the annual rate of inflation is 20 percent, the real yield would be −3 percent. Negative yields always lead to a flight of capital and investments out of the country. The result will be a collapsing currency even though nominal interest rates are extremely high.

Monetary Policy Direction

The primary tool used in monetary policy is changes to benchmark interest rates. Here in the United States that is the Federal Funds Rate. Across the pond in Europe, the European Central Bank uses the Refinance Rate for the eurozone. Any change in interest rates effectively amounts to changes in the cost of capital or money. Higher interest rates increase the cost of borrowing, while lower interest rates reduce the cost of borrowing.

This sets up a chain of events. The benchmark rates set by central banks apply to the nation's overall banking system and as such will also determine the cost of borrowing between banks as well. Banks in turn will now adjust rates they charge to corporations and to individual borrowers based on these benchmark rates; thus there is nowhere to hide. Monetary policy falls into one of two camps: restrictive and expansionary. Let's look at both.

Restrictive Policy. On Wall Street, restrictive monetary policy is known as "tighter monetary policy" or for short simply "tightening." Here is how it works. Higher interest rates increase the cost of borrowing. When borrowing costs go higher, spending and investment go lower, and the economy slows down. Central banks will use tighter monetary policy when they think their economy is expanding too much too soon. The concern of the central bank is that rising demand along with the low cost of borrowing could lead to inflation beyond acceptable levels. Think too much money chasing too few goods.

Expansionary Policy. On the flip side of things, expansionary monetary policy, referred to on Wall Street as "accommodative," is achieved through lowering interest rates, which reduces the cost of borrowing, which will increase spending and investing, making the economy stronger. An accommodative monetary policy is employed when economic growth is low or contracting, usually signaled by rising unemployment.

There may be no investment vehicle anywhere in the world quite like the currency markets, where you can make money and lose money, lots of it, in the blink of an eye.

🐜 ANT Valorem

- The U.S. dollar is on one side or another of 90 percent of all currency market transactions.
- Interest rates are critical for currencies because they drive the ultimate direction of the global flow of all capital.
- The currency market is the most volatile as it overreacts to almost every single economic data point.
- Always remember it's one country's interest rates in relation to another country's interest rates that matter the most.
- Remember it is more important to focus on "real" interest rates.

CHAPTER FOUR

Get Real

INVESTING IN REAL ESTATE

Real estate is at the core of almost every business, and it's certainly at the core of most people's wealth. In order to build your wealth and improve your business smarts, you need to know about real estate.

—Donald Trump

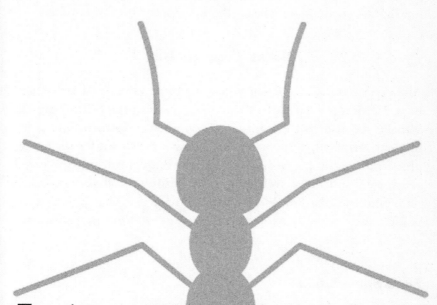

In real estate investing, there is much more to it than the old "location, location, location" joke. While location is important, it is not the only thing that is important. Actually it is a confluence of three issues that will determine the success of your real estate investment. The first is location; the second is what possible real estate uses can be put on that location; the third and last is what the local land use and zoning ordinances allow currently and what they likely are to allow.

Always keep in perspective these guidelines regarding the location of your real estate investment. There is no such thing as the perfect real estate location for every type of real estate use. Think about this objectively for a minute. The best place to put a restaurant may not be the best place to put a gas station, and it may or may not work for a medical office complex. The building of a brand-new fire station or police station is clearly a sign of progress and development; however, it may not do anything to enhance the value of the land around it.

What Type to Buy

After you have decided that you want to invest in real estate, the next decision is what type of real estate you want to buy. There are actually six principal categories of real estate investing: land speculation; farmland; residential, both single-family and multifamily properties; retail shops and shopping; commercial and industrial properties; and hotel and lodging. Let's look at all six beginning with land speculation. As I review all these principal categories, I point out both the benefits and the weaknesses or costs associated with each of these real estate categories.

Land Speculation

In its most basic form, land speculation is simply an investment in land with the hope that it will increase enough in value to cover the cost to hold it and provide a profit over and above what you initially paid for it. While this sounds simple, it is not. Land speculation requires the highest degree of due diligence of any of the real estate investment categories. The reason it is called "speculation" is you must decide on what you think the type and pattern of growth is going to be in the community; then you must sync that up with current and proposed infrastructure projects on the drawing board of the various state and local government agencies.

The benefit of land speculation is that it stands to provide you with the greatest upside of all real estate investments. The thought is that if you start with vacant land, which has the lowest of all basic value along the real estate hierarchy, and move it up that hierarchy to a commercial real estate site, you have taken your investment from the bottom of the real estate food chain to the top, so to speak, and everything in between just turned into pure profit. When the landscape and circumstances are favorable to land investment, there is really very little risk that your investment will not one day finally pay off—that is as long as you have the time and financial wherewithal to hold that land. The single most important issue to land speculation is being able to successfully assess the potential growth patterns of the local area by making sure that you have a good handle on the future developments that are currently on the drawing board.

One potential cost or weakness in land speculation is that more times than not local governments change their mind and decide not to proceed with their future plans. This could be for political reasons when newly elected local officials have a different view of things. Or it could be for budgetary reasons as the local government decides to dramatically pull back on all spending. I witnessed this firsthand when I was the youngest city manager ever in the state of Ohio. Back then, the on-again off-again decision in Beavercreek, Ohio, to build a research park and a shopping mall caused the vacant land around those two proposed projects to skyrocket and collapse, depending on the political winds of the day.

Another problem, in addition to simply changing plans at the drop of a hat and deciding not to do the project at all, is the decision to amend plans. This happens all the time. Let's say local government decides to move the proposed new bridge a mile farther north on the river. This means that your 100-acre raw land tract is now not going to have the instant access across the river to the other side of town. Also, moving the bridge to a different part of town creates a new area of attention and focus.

The longer the holding period or time of speculation for the raw land, the more difficult it is to make money. That is because the longer you hold it the more expensive it becomes to hold it, all things being equal. The problem, however, is that all things are never equal. There is a very good chance that the taxes on your land speculation investment will double and then double again depending on how long you hold the investment. Also, look out for this time bomb: Local governments can impose a building moratorium that can limit any and all developments until basic utilities are brought to the site. The cost of those utilities, by the way, can be charged as a cost to the property owner. Now the cost of carrying your land speculation investment just got a whole lot more expensive.

Farmland

Let's move on to our second of six principal real estate categories: farmland. Here is an interesting perspective to think about. You can actually combine land speculation, which I just discussed, along with farmland—using the exact same piece of real estate.

What I like about farmland is that the land itself is valuable and can produce a strong cash flow. You must, however, do your financial homework. Most farmland has a high maintenance cost. Farming has come a long way and today is considered big business. Like any business, an investor getting into farming must clearly understand the risks and rewards of that business.

You must remember that not all farmland brings with it a high maintenance cost. Different uses of the farmland for different products bring with them a different cycle of preparation, planting, and harvesting.

Various types of tree farms are a great example. Some tree farms grow trees to be used in landscaping. These tree farms have limited preparation but require years and years of growth until the first batch of trees are big enough to be sold for landscaping. However, once the process begins, the rotation of selling some trees while others are at various stages of growth can provide a steady flow of income.

Tree farming can also produce wood for furniture or construction, or wood pulp for paper and other chemical products. This type of tree farm has the longest time between planting and harvesting because these trees need to be very large and very mature. This type of tree farm gives a land speculator a chance to double down, similar to a bonus. When the owners sell their land and the trees must be cleared for development, they are not only paid for the land but also paid for the trees that they just cut down.

A cattle ranch or sheep ranch has similar benefits because the cattle or sheep living on the land can be sold off at anytime once the economic and market conditions signal that it is time to sell the land.

The real benefit of buying farmland is if you intend to use it for just that, farmland. Nonfarmers (most investors) are purchasing farmland in the hope that one day it will be used for something other than farmland. If you are buying farmland to be used as farmland, you don't have to worry about some day getting the zoning changed so that you can use that farmland for something else later down the line.

The cost or challenge of investing in farmland is clear. If the final strategy is to sell the farmland to a developer, you have just added one more prerequisite for success. As farmland becomes more and more scarce, you run the risk of a trend in development where local officials want to keep any property that is farmland to remain farmland. That would mean that changing the use of the farmland may require court action. This may cause yet another layer of cost, which will eat into your farmland real estate investment profit.

Residential: Single-Family Homes

Let's now move on to our third of six principal real estate investment categories: residential. There are actually two subsets to residential real estate: single-family homes and multifamily properties. I touch on both beginning with single-family homes.

ANTs

Real estate investing by buying single-family homes is the most popular of all real estate investments. That is because there are three different strategies you can use to do this. You can buy it, live in it, improve it over time, and then sell it. The second strategy is to buy it, fix it up right away, and then sell it. The third strategy is to simply buy it and rent it.

One of the greatest benefits of investing in single-family homes is that single-family home sellers are always the most motivated of all sellers. That is because there is an almost endless list of reasons why people may need to sell their single-family home and do it now. Maybe it is because they need a larger home and they need it now due to the arrival of a child and the growth of their family. On the flip side, maybe they need a smaller home due to shrinkage in the size of their family. Maybe their children are grown and gone, or there could have been the death of a family member or even a divorce. Many times these highly motivated sellers are driven by employment issues. Being transferred to a new work location or taking a new job in a new city are two such examples. There is also the possibility of financial problems where the current owners can no longer afford the property, or the seller may just need to raise cash for another investment opportunity, and the best way to raise cash is to sell the house.

Everything is not always rosy with single-family home real estate investments. First, if you are looking for a quick turnaround to make a fast investment dollar, this would not be the way to do it. Another downside to be aware of is that many investors think they want to be major landlords and build their fortune and income stream by buying and then renting out all of these single-family homes. Most landlords quickly discover that the ongoing property maintenance cost and problems that come with owning multiple single-family homes is probably not worth the time, effort, money, or headaches.

Let me give you some advice on this so-called form of investment. The only time I would suggest buying a single-family home and then renting it is to buy you time. What are you buying time for? You are buying time until the real estate market improves. While you are buying time, you can also make any improvements or enhancements necessary to better sell this property. But best of all, the cash flow (or rent) from your tenant is paying you to wait.

Residential: Multifamily Properties

Let's shift gears here and focus on the other subset of residential real estate: multifamily properties. Multifamily properties cover a rather wide spectrum of real estate. In its most basic form, any property that has more than one family unit is considered a multifamily property. So under that broad definition, the smallest would be a duplex (two units), and the largest could be hundreds or thousands of units.

This is a new dynamic for investors. Unlike what we have previously discussed, land speculation, farmland, and single-family homes where the financing is focused solely on the individual investor's financial strength, multifamily properties are focused on cash flow. In this scenario lenders will still look at the investors' financial strength; however, that is secondary. What they are really focused on is the income this investment will produce.

All multifamily rental properties ultimately succeed or fail for one simple reason: cash flow. Cash flow and the need for it drive everything. Think of it from this perspective: If there is a shortage of rental units in a given area and the vacancy rates are close to zero, it enables you the owners to be extremely selective about the type of tenant you are willing to rent to.

While on the surface this may appear somewhat subjective, it is also very important. The type of tenant you allow in your property will have a great deal to do with the trend either up or down that your property is about to embark upon. Maybe if we look at the other side of the coin the problem will be easier to spot. Let's say there is a rather dramatic shift in the rental market in which there is an extreme shortage of tenants. Under that scenario, you the owner, can no longer be selective because you are dependent on their cash flow to pay your mortgage payments and to upkeep the property. If they have a pulse, you rent the property to them. You can see that when the type of tenant falls so may the value of the property.

This is not rocket science here. In fact, it is extremely easy to do your own research, because everything is out in the open. One of the great investment aspects of the rental market is that there are no secrets. Just get in your car and drive around the community, go on the Internet, or grab a community paper and look at the classified ads. You can make your own list of rental properties that have vacancies. If they are cutting rents or keeping them stable, that will let you know how selective property managers are in acquiring their tenants. If rent is on the rise that means the selection is tight. That almost always means that there is a shortage of rental units, which in turn is creating a potential investment opportunity.

The benefit of owning residential multifamily property is clear. You can simply sit back and let the cash flow from your properties pay off your mortgage. It takes time, but it works and because multifamily properties serve such a basic and important need, it helps to prevent your downside risk.

Think about rental properties. What they actually do is to provide housing and shelter to those who cannot afford or may be choosing not to buy a single-family home at this time. This market has a constant ebb and flow. There will always be residents moving both to and from home ownership. Some residents may be improving and upgrading their living conditions, while others are being forced into less-expensive living arrangements.

Like any investment there is always a downside. The major downside is usually the time-intensive management problems that come with dealing with tenants. It gets back to what I said earlier: One key to minimal management problems is the selection of tenants.

Retail Shops and Shopping

Let's move on to the fourth principal category of real estate investing: retail shops and shopping. Did you ever notice how retail shopping centers are everywhere? In good economic times and in bad economic times, the only thing we can truly count on is that new shopping centers will be built even though many current shopping centers are almost vacant.

A typical business district in every town will have individual shops lining the streets filled with restaurants, sundry shops, clothing stores, and coffee shops, just to name a few. Finding retail shops and shopping centers is very easy. First, the areas are always built on major streets or highways, which make them easy to find. Many of these buildings are for sale, even though there is no for sale sign. The reason for this is that most property owners do not want to let their tenants know the property is up for sale.

One clear advantage about retail shops and shopping real estate investments is that it is relatively easy to see the trends and the traffic flows. You don't have to be a real estate guru to tell which areas are improving and which areas are falling into decline. Selecting the right property to buy depends solely on your ability to deal with the complexity of renting out retail shops or shopping center spaces.

Let me give you an important piece of advice. Buying a large retail space is not for the novice investor. The only way that I would consider suggesting that a novice investor get involved is if there is sufficient cash flow to hire a property manager with shopping center management experience. Little strip malls, however, are another story and are actually a good way to start. The reason is that these buildings are almost always in need of repair. They can be easily remodeled to upgrade both the look and the rent. This becomes a very easy way to improve the cash flow of your investment. The best benefit of this type of real estate investment is the fact that it serves a basic need in the community. That need could be eating, shopping, or dry cleaning. If you have chosen your location well, you should not have a problem with high vacancies.

> *One clear advantage about retail shops and shopping real estate investments is that it is relatively easy to see the trends and the traffic flows.*

Once again, the main downside of this real estate investment is dealing with the tenants. Are you noticing a theme here? It is critical to be as selective as possible and to upgrade your tenants at every opportunity. Do not give into the temptation to fill a vacant space with a less than ideal tenant. It will be the single biggest mistake that you make. The first mistake would be by lowering your standards and allowing in the wrong kind of tenant, which causes the second mistake by starting a downhill slide that will most likely cause other vacancies to occur.

Commercial and Industrial Properties

The fifth principal category of real estate investing is commercial and industrial properties. Commercial and industrial properties cover a wide spectrum. They go from office buildings to warehouses and anything and everything in between. One way to think of it is like this: If the property is a building that is not used for habitation, it is commercial or industrial property.

Both commercial and industrial properties fall into two categories: single use and multiuse. Let's say for example that Procter and Gamble occupies an entire building. That is clearly a single tenant

(Procter and Gamble), but the use could be multiple use because they could use some for offices, some for warehousing, medical facilities, and even restaurants. This is a big difference from a single tenant with a single purpose like a cafeteria restaurant. This also is a single tenant, but the use is limited to one thing, a cafeteria restaurant, unless there is a major remodeling.

Unlike the Procter and Gamble example above, you will find that most multiuse buildings are also multitenant buildings. Multitenant buildings have the benefit of spreading the obligation of the rent over several or many different tenants. Now that doesn't mean that having a single tenant is bad. If your single tenant is financially strong and has a top tier credit rating, your single-tenant building is more attractive than multitenant buildings. The one glaring problem with a single-tenant building is when the single-tenant building is vacant it goes from 100 percent occupied to zero percent occupied.

In the world of commercial or industrial properties, your tenant is often a net tenant or a triple net tenant. When a tenant is a net tenant or triple net tenant, you are passing on other expenses and costs to the tenant over and above the actual rent. Let me alert you to something: The terms *net* and *triple net* are not universal in their meanings. You as a prospective investor need to obtain an exact definition of the other obligations tenants are expected to pay. Do not make a mistake and assume that your triple net tenant pays everything.

Triple net tenants are tenants that pay rent, all building maintenance, taxes, and insurance. Others even go beyond that and include all other costs that may be assessed against the property. In this case, the cost to your tenant is established as if the tenant actually owned the property. This is the situation you want to find, because in this case your financial investment will require very little if any management.

The clear benefit of investing in commercial and industrial properties is the ease of operation and management. But just like all cash flow income properties, the income stream will be the number one factor in determining the value of your investment, and it will also determine the basis for your mortgage financing. The home run that you need to look for here is to take over a property that will need little improvement and can be converted to a higher cash flow stream. That is how the really big money is made in commercial and industrial investing.

> *When a tenant is a net tenant or triple net tenant, you are passing on other expenses and costs to the tenant over and above the actual rent.*

So how do you lose money? Clearly time is not on your side. In fact, time is your biggest problem. There is a big time lag that occurs in the development of this type of property. Think about this: You find a major shortage of office space or commercial building so you decide to build one. In the time from your idea until the finished product is ready for its first tenant years may pass. In that timeframe this shortage could turn into overcapacity before you are even done. Or even worse, if during that timeframe, there is an economic downturn the demand could have a major downturn as well.

The second major problem is there is no such thing anymore as a risk-free tenant. Even some of the biggest and best corporations in the country have fallen on hard times. At one point these companies were thought to be risk free if you got one as a tenant. Just think of Enron, WorldCom, and Arthur Andersen to name a few.

Hotel and Lodging

The sixth and final principal category of real estate investing is hotel and lodging. Maybe the real estate investment that touches every aspect around the globe is hotel and lodging. The reason is that hotels and motels cater to every single demographic aspect representing all walks of life. The proof of that would be room rates that run from $20 a night to over $2,000 a night. This industry also goes through major swings in development.

The middle-ground hotels are usually not what we refer to as full-service properties and have few if any amenities for their customers. These are what we refer to as "sleep and leave" hotels and what are sometimes called "interstate properties." They fill up every night but are empty every morning. As you can imagine, this type of turnover will create inherent management problems.

This is clearly the riskiest of all real estate investments. The reason is that you have no control over your competition. Think of it this way: The ideal location for a new hotel would be at the intersection of two major interstate highways that is only a two-hour drive from three or four major metropolitan areas that all have multiple colleges and universities. This would be the perfect spot for a new hotel. The problem is every other hotel franchise came to the same conclusion that you did. That's why this real estate asset class is so challenging.

Here is where the best opportunities are global in nature. Think about competition from this perspective: In the United States, we have a population of 300 million, and we have 4.5 million hotel rooms. In India their population is 1.1 billion, and they have 105,000 hotel rooms. Where do you think the opportunity might be? Go global, go global, and go even more global!

How to Invest in Real Estate

Now that you know the principal real estate categories to invest in, I bring this chapter to a close by focusing on how you can invest in real estate. Actually there are three major options. The first is quite obvious, which is simply the outright purchase of the real estate property. The second option is something we refer to on Wall Street as a REIT, which stands for real estate investment trust. The third and final option is another acronym we have on Wall Street called an ETF, which stands for exchange-traded fund. I want to focus on the latter two options, real estate investment trusts and exchange-traded funds for real estate.

Real Estate Investment Trust (REIT)

A real estate investment trust, or REIT, is an investment company that pools investment money from many individuals to buy and manage real estate while also providing an open market for shares. REIT shares can be bought or sold through your financial adviser just as you can buy or sell a share of stock through your financial adviser.

REITs by law are not allowed to pass on any tax benefits to you as an individual investor. Even if there happen to be losses, they will not be treated as tax deductible. As a result of this, a REIT's management has every motive to make sure that it reports profits and positive cash flow. Thus, for any of you reading this book who do not want to manage real estate investment holdings directly and who are not investing for some tax advantage benefit, the REIT is your single best choice, especially when you overlay the fact that you can buy or sell it daily on the open market.

Basically, a REIT is simply a pool of investor capital. You can buy the REIT shares from your financial adviser at the time the program is first formed. After that, shares can be bought or sold at any time through your financial adviser. The current daily values of each REIT are listed in the financial press in the exact same way stocks are listed, and just like stocks REITs are traded publicly.

Thus the REIT is designed to generate cash profits to you, its investors, as well as providing management services to them. The REIT's purpose of cash flow, which is passive income, is far better in our current tax climate than negative cash flow and worthless passive losses. How are profits paid? All profits are paid in the form of dividends. The REIT is required by law to pass through no less than 95 percent of its profits.

The best way to think of a REIT is as a mutual fund that specializes in real estate rather than stocks or bonds. In fact, many of the same rules apply in terms of organization, reporting, disclosure, regulatory oversight, and liability. When you look for a REIT investment, make sure you understand the difference between the two major classifications of REITs:

REITs That Own: REITs that actually own the real estate are called equity REITs. Equity REITs are designed to buy property and hold it for current income as well as future price appreciation in real estate market value. The trust itself is the legal owner of the property, and each shareholder in turn owns shares of the trust. That means the status of a REIT investor is the same as that of a corporate shareholder.

REITs That Lend: REITs that lend are called mortgage REITs. The mortgage REIT takes no equity position but instead funds development of projects or the purchases of existing projects. Mortgage REITs have given the entire REIT assets class a black eye. Back in the early 1970s several mortgage REITs loaned excessively to developers to build projects; however, most of those projects never got built. I have never been a big fan of mortgage REITs.

The best way to think of a REIT is as a mutual fund that specializes in real estate rather than stocks or bonds.

Real Estate Exchange-Traded Funds (ETFs)

The exchange-traded fund (or ETF) is a mutual fund designed to specialize in an industry, a commodity, currency, country, or some other specialized focus. In this case, it is real estate. One of the great advantages mutual funds have always had over stocks is the automatic diversification and professional management that funds offer.

The real estate ETF mutual fund has a predetermined portfolio representing a cross section of the real estate industry. This basket of stocks, so to speak, does not need to be managed or changed so management fees are never a factor in picking an ETF as they are with traditional funds. Again the ETF trades just like a stock. You will have capital gains or losses from ETF investing, and they will be treated like any stock trade or bond trade.

Just like stocks, ETF shares are bought and sold on the public exchange through your financial adviser. This makes the real estate ETF the most liquid way to invest in real estate, and if you compare it to direct real estate ownership, it is a diversified and extremely liquid investment with no ongoing cash flow problems.

The actual portfolio of a real estate ETF may include shares of publicly traded real estate companies, REITs, and other organizations in the United States, internationally, or globally. This diversification may also include land, farmland, residential (both single-family and multifamily properties), retail shops and shopping, commercial and industrial properties, and hotel and lodging. It can also have other equity or mortgage-based REIT products. Looked at another way, you can find a real estate ETF to achieve any real estate investment strategy you may have.

ANT Valorem

- Land speculation provides you with the greatest upside of all real estate investments.
- One of the great benefits about single-family home sellers is they are typically the most motivated of all real estate sellers.
- The added advantage to retail shops and shopping real estate is that it usually serves a basic need in the community.
- Stay away: Hotel and lodging real estate is the riskiest of all.
- The best way to invest in real estate is through a real estate investment trust ETF.

CHAPTER FIVE

The Bridge to Everywhere

INVESTING IN INFRASTRUCTURE

The wise man bridges the gap by laying out the path by means of which he can get from where he is to where he wants to go.
            —John Pierpont Morgan, American financier

Before we can invest in something, we better first clearly understand exactly what it is. Infrastructure consists of the basic physical structures that are needed to operate any civilization. Think roads, bridges, water and sewer pipes, telecommunications, and airports.

From an economic perspective, a civilization cannot develop without infrastructure. The reason is that a country's infrastructure provides the necessary vehicle to assist in the movement of goods and services. Without it the economy cannot grow, and if the economy does not grow, the civilization will not survive.

Think about it this way: Commodities are shipped across the ocean and arrive at a seaport, which is part of a country's infrastructure. These commodities are then taken via railroad, which is also part of a country's infrastructure, to a manufacturing facility.

At the same time, new parts that are needed at the manufacturing facility have arrived at the airport, which is also part of a country's infrastructure. Once the manufacturing is completed, these products are loaded on a truck for distribution to consumers, and these trucks travel on highways that are part of the infrastructure. Every bridge that is used is yet another form of infrastructure. From this perspective, infrastructure may be the single most important factor in a civilization's success.

The Road Starts with . . . Roads

The most basic form of infrastructure, roads, has the longest history. The very first paved streets were built in the city of Ur, which was a coastal city near the mouth of the Euphrates River on the Persian Gulf. Roads were built there in 4000 B.C. Corduroy roads, which were made by placing sand-covered logs perpendicular to the direction of the road, were built in Glastonbury, England, in 3300 B.C. Brick-paved roads were built by the Indus Valley civilization on the Indian subcontinent around 3000 B.C. In 500 B.C., Darius the Great started an extensive road system for Persia (now modern-day Iran), which included the Persian Royal Road, stretching from Susa to Sardis and covering 1,677 miles. Horseback couriers could now make the trip in seven days. It was, in fact, this exact road that led the Greek historian Herodotus to write about these Persian couriers riding on the Persian Royal Road: "Neither snow, nor rain, nor heat, nor darkness of night prevents these couriers from completing their designated stages with utmost speed." As another slice of history, that quote served as the inspiration for the unofficial motto of the United States Postal Service.

Fast-forward to modern-day history; in 1925, Italy became the first country to build a freeway-like road, called the Autostrada dei Laghi, which linked Milan to Lake Como. Soon after, Germany created their autobahns, which were the first limited-access high-speed road network in the entire world. The first section from Frankfurt to Darmstadt opened in 1935. The first long-distance freeway in the United States was the Pennsylvania Turnpike, which opened on October 1, 1940.

Types of Infrastructure

All infrastructure can be classified into five types: transportation, energy, water, waste management, and communications. Think of infrastructure as anything that moves people, vehicles, fluids, energy, or information. I briefly touch on all five beginning with transportation.

Transportation

Maybe the most recognizable of all infrastructures is in the transportation area, which includes roads and highways, bridges and tunnels. Transportation infrastructure also includes the electrical system to support these roads, both streetlights and traffic lights. Mass transit systems are also a part of transportation infrastructure, including subways, tramways, commuter rail systems, trolleys, and bus transportation. Railways are also included along with their rail yards, train stations and terminal facilities, level crossings, signaling, and communication systems.

Airports, seaports, canals, and ferries are part of the infrastructure network. While many people don't think about them in this light, bicycle paths, pedestrian walkways, sidewalks, and even curbs are all considered infrastructure.

Energy

Let's move on to energy infrastructure, beginning with oil. This includes all petroleum pipelines, including storage and distribution terminals, and oil wells, along with all refineries, tanker ships, and truck fleets. The same can be said for natural gas, which includes its pipelines, storage, and distribution terminals, making up its local distribution network. All gas wells and the fleet of ships and trucks transporting liquefied gas are part of infrastructure.

Getting back to energy basics, let's think steam or hot water production and distribution networks for district heating systems. Coal mines as well as specialized facilities for storing and transporting coal are included. Finally, the entire electrical power network is classified as infrastructure, which includes all generation plants, the entire electric grid, every substation, and the entire end user local distribution system.

Water

Let's move on to the third type of infrastructure: water. This begins with our drinking water and includes the mass network and system of water pipes, storage reservoirs, and treatment facilities. In those treatment facilities think filtration, pumps, and valves. At the end of the distribution system, you have a water meter, which is also part of the infrastructure network. The same can be said for waste water as was said for water infrastructure; however, here we are collecting and disposing of the water. Drainage systems, such as storm sewers and even ditches, are a form of infrastructure. Taking that drainage to the next level, we would have our major flood control systems like dikes, levees, and floodgates.

Waste Management

The fourth type of infrastructure is waste management. It begins with the municipal garbage and recyclable collection operation, and ends in one of two facilities: either a solid waste incinerator or a solid waste landfill. In between those two bookends we find material recovery facilities. One final component of waste management infrastructure, which is also one of the fastest-growing areas, is hazardous waste disposal facilities.

Communications

Fifth and finally, we have the massive and complex communications infrastructure. It begins with "snail mail," so named because of how slow it is. This has become the new nickname for the postal service, but the postal service as well as all sorting facilities is a form of infrastructure. From snail mail, we move on to e-mail and the entire Internet, which includes high-speed data cables, routers, and servers as well as the protocols. It also includes the basic software required for the system to function.

Next are both television and radio transmission stations as well as cable television's physical networks, including the receiving stations and the massive local distribution networks. The telephone system using landlines, including all of the switching systems, is infrastructure, as is the entire mobile phone network.

Also included are a couple of things that we never see because they are either too high or too low: communication satellites and undersea cables.

Finally don't forget about the dedicated government telecommunications network such as those used by the military or emergency services.

Why Invest?

Now that we know exactly what infrastructure is, you still may be thinking, *Why should I invest in it?* Two reasons come to mind. The first should be quite obvious to savvy investors. There are very high barriers to entry, which in turn make direct competition difficult.

Just think about the cost of building a new airport or a water treatment plant to compete with an existing one. They are all physical assets, and they are localized. You can't outsource your airport or water treatment plant to India or Pakistan. What this means is that infrastructure assets are much less susceptible to the natural competition that is faced daily in every other industry.

Second, because almost all infrastructure assets are economic necessities, they usually have very predictable revenue streams. These predictable revenue streams do two things. First, they provide a great source of long-term income, and second they are one of the reasons that infrastructure investments have relatively low volatility.

> *Infrastructure assets are much less susceptible to the natural competition that is faced daily in every other industry.*

How to Invest

There are basically two ways to invest in this infrastructure investment theme. The first is in mature developed economies and markets, like the United States, that must embark on a massive infrastructure spending program in order to improve and repair its outdated and aging infrastructure.

The second way to invest is in emerging and developing countries like China that are being forced to quickly build and create their infrastructure.

America's Aging Infrastructure

The American Society of Civil Engineers (ASCE) conducts a study every two years grading America's infrastructure from A to F, called the "Report Card for America's Infrastructure." The most recent study gives the United States a "D." It will need to spend $2.2 trillion over the next five years to get its infrastructure to an acceptable level.

Here are just a few of the highlights or, should I say, lowlights. In the area of aviation, the Federal Aviation Administration predicts an annual 3 percent growth rate in travel. Air travelers are already faced with increasing delays and inadequate conditions as a result of the long overdue need to modernize the outdated air traffic control system. Aviation grade was a "D."

In the area of roads, Americans spend 4.2 billion hours a year stuck in traffic at a cost to the economy of $78 billion or $710 per motorist. Poor road conditions cost motorists $67 billion a year in repairs and 14,000 Americans their lives. One-third of America's major roads are in poor or mediocre condition and 36 percent of major urban highways are congested. The grade for roads was a "D−."

In the area of bridges, more than 26 percent or one in four, are either structurally deficient or functionally obsolete. The grade for bridges was a "C."

In the area of water, America's drinking water systems face an annual shortfall of $11 billion a year to replace aging facilities that are near the end of their useful life. Many of these facilities do not comply with existing water regulations giving them little if any chance to comply with future ones. This doesn't even account for any growth in the demand for water over the next 20 years. Also, leaking pipes lose an estimated 7 billion gallons of clean drinking water a day. The grade for water was a "D−."

In the area of dams, as dams age and downstream development soars, the risk skyrockets. The number of deficient dams has risen to more than 4,000 including 1,819 high hazard-potential dams. Over the past six years, for every deficient high hazard-potential dam repaired, two more were declared deficient. Do the math—we can't win this race. There are over 85,000 dams in the United States, and the average age is just over 51 years. Dams received a grade of "D."

In the area of levees, more than 85 percent of the nation's estimated 100,000 miles of levees are locally owned and maintained. The reliability of many of these levees is unknown, and many are over 50 years old and were originally built to protect crops from flooding. With a huge increase in development behind all of these levees, the risk to public health and safety from failure has gone through the roof. The grade given to levees is a "D–."

Finally, in the area of inland waterways, there are 257 locks still in use in the nation's inland waterways. Thirty were built in the 1800s, and another 92 are more than 60 years old. The average age of all federally owned or operated locks is 60 years; meanwhile the planned design life for these locks is only 50 years.

This really should not surprise anyone who has traveled across the United States. Every day it seems we get a new reminder, like the I-35 bridge that collapsed in Minneapolis. According to the U.S. Department of Transportation, 756 steel-deck truss bridges span America's waterways, just like the one in Minnesota, and most of these were built in the 1950s with 11 percent of these bridges having the same weakness that caused the I-35 bridge collapse in Minneapolis.

Instead of focusing all resources on fixing the problem, politicians are still busy crafting pork barrel infrastructure projects for their constituents back home. Maybe there is no better example than the "bridge to nowhere" in Alaska. It was going to connect the town of Ketchikan, with a population of 8,900, to its airport on Gravina Island with a population less than 50, not counting seals and bald eagles!

> *There are 257 locks still in use in the nation's inland waterways. Thirty were built in the 1800s and another 92 are more than 60 years old.*

There are two direct ways to invest in the aging infrastructure in America. One is with a company called Olin Corporation. Olin has two major business segments, one of which is chlor-alkali. In fact, the company is the third-largest producer of chlor-alkali products, which are critical to the treatment of water. Olin has been involved in the U.S. chlor-alkali industry for more than 100 years and manufactures chlorine and caustic soda, sodium hydrosulfite, hydrochloric acid, hydrogen, potassium hydroxide, and bleach products. Their ticker symbol on the New York Stock Exchange is "OLN."

The second direct way to invest is with a company called Sterling Construction Company. It specializes in the building, reconstruction, and repair of transportation and water infrastructure. Transportation projects include highways, roads, bridges, light rail, and commuter rail. Water infrastructure projects include water, wastewater, and storm drainage systems. Its ticker symbol on the NASDAQ is "STRL.O."

Go Global

While the opportunities for infrastructure investing in the United States seem limitless, outside the United States the opportunities are even better, especially in the emerging market economies and countries like China. The reason is urbanization. As the world becomes more urbanized, the infrastructure will be forced to catch up. The United Nations expects the world's population to expand from its current level of 6.8 billion to 8.3 billion by 2030, according to the *Demographic Yearbook*. In 2030, fully 60 percent of that population will be living in urban areas. Here's a shocking comparison for you: In 1900 only 13 percent of the world's population lived in urban areas.

Nowhere is that urbanization more dramatic than in China. While the urbanization of China is a long-term trend, something that has been occurring for a long time, it is still nothing short of amazing. It is the single largest shift in history, with people leaving the rural agricultural areas to migrate into the urbanized areas.

It is unprecedented. Already 500 million people have migrated, or have been urbanized, in the past 50 years. By the year 2025, it is estimated that more than 900 million people will have been urbanized in China, a number that is three times larger than the entire population of the United States.

According to the CIA's *World Factbook*, here's how this shift has evolved: In 1950, China had 552 million people; 490 million lived in rural areas, and 62 million (11.2 percent) lived in urban areas. By 1975, China had a population of 962 million people; 790 million lived in rural areas, and 172 million (17.8 percent) lived in urban areas. In 2005, China's population stood at 1,307 billion; 745 million living in rural areas, and 562 million (42.9 percent) living in urban areas. (That 562 million now living in urban areas is larger than the entire population of China was in 1950.)

It is projected that in 2025, China's population will be 1,427 billion people, with 467 million living in rural areas and 960 million (67.2 percent) living in urban areas. It is unprecedented to shift your urban population from 11.2 percent to 67.2 percent in only 75 years. Here is the best way to think about this urbanization in China: It would be like everyone in Texas deciding to move to Houston.

All of this urbanization will require clean water, reliable energy, efficient public transportation, and dependable communications networks. In other words, it needs infrastructure.

Here is the best way to think about this urbanization in China: it would be like everyone in Texas deciding to move to Houston.

In almost every country, including the United States, which came along kicking and screaming, there has been a move toward government privatization of big ticket infrastructure assets. It is this global privatization that creates investment opportunities in infrastructure. The most popular infrastructure assets to privatize are roads, toll roads, seaports, and airports. Let me give you an investment opportunity in each of these privatization categories beginning with toll roads.

Jiangsu Expressway Company. The first investment opportunity is a company called Jiangsu Expressway Company Limited. They are engaged in the investment, construction, operation, and management of the Jiangsu section of the Shanghai-Nanjing Expressway and other toll highways within Jiangsu Province. In addition, the company also develops passenger transportation and other ancillary services along all of these highways like gas stations for refueling, along with full service for automobile repair and maintenance, food and catering, and retail shops as well as hotels and motels for lodging.

Apart from the Shanghai-Nanjing Expressway, the company also owns other interests, in whole or in part, in other toll roads and bridges located in Jiangsu Province, including the Shanghai-Nanjing Section of G312, the Nanjing section of the Nanjing-Lianyungang Highway, the Xicheng Expressway, the Guangjing Expressway, the

Jiangyin Yangtze Bridge, and the Sujiahang Expressway. The stock is traded over the counter (OTC) under the symbol "JEXYY."

Shenzhen Chiwan Wharf Holdings. In the category of seaport operators we have a company called Shenzhen Chiwan Wharf Holdings. They are principally engaged in the handling, storage, transportation, and other related services of containers and bulk cargo as well as tugboat services and shipping. The company's bulk cargo business mainly handles cereals and fertilizer. Remember my feed-the-world commodity investment theme in Chapter 2? This is the infrastructure investment theme to move all of those commodities to feed the world. Its shares are traded in China (A Shares) under the symbol: "SHE:000022."

Fraport AG. The third and final category is in the area of airport operators. The best investment idea here is a German company called Fraport AG who owns and operates the Frankfurt International Airport. Fraport developed the Frankfurt Airport to the "Frankfurt Airport City," offering all amenities including shopping, lodging, restaurants, and parking.

It is a global infrastructure powerhouse with investments in 60 different facilities all over Europe and on four continents. Here are just a few of the highlights by country:

- Egypt: where they have 100 percent ownership of the Cairo International Airport.
- Senegal (Africa): where they have a 10 percent ownership of the Leopold Sedar Senghor International Airport and provide consulting services.
- India: where they have a 10 percent ownership in the Indira Gandhi International Airport.

- Turkey: where they have a 51 percent ownership in the Antalya Airport.
- Saudi Arabia: where they have a 100 percent ownership in both the King Abdulaziz International Airport and the King Khalid International Airport.
- Bulgaria: where they have a 60 percent ownership in both the Burgas Airport and the Varna Airport.
- Peru: where they have a 100 percent ownership of the Jorge Chávez International Airport.
- Russia: where they have a 35.5 percent ownership in the Pulkovo Airport.
- China: where they have a 24.5 percent ownership in the Xi'an Xianyang International Airport.

The stock is listed on both the Xetra and the Frankfurt Stock Exchanges under the ticker symbol "FRA."

China Boom. China alone is expected to account for almost 30 percent of global infrastructure spending over the next two decades. China is an infrastructure game-changer. You can throw away any reference to historical infrastructure supply and demand trends, as China's voracious infrastructure demand is creating a new world order. China is expected to spend an almost unheard of $35 trillion in the next 20 years on infrastructure.

If you want a piece of that investment action, here is how to get it. Emerging Global Shares launched a China Infrastructure Index (CHXX) that tracks a diversified basket of Chinese infrastructure outfits. This is a great way to play both China and infrastructure with the same investment.

ANT Valorem

- Invest both ways in infrastructure, in mature developed markets that need infrastructure repair and the evolving, underdeveloped markets that need to build infrastructure.
- One way to invest in water in the United States is with a company called Olin (OLN), one of the largest producers of products critical to the treatment of water.
- An investment in Sterling Construction Company (STRL.O) will get you exposure to both transportation and water infrastructure in the United States.
- Fraport AG (FRA) gets your infrastructure exposure in 60 different facilities all over Europe and on four continents, including its legacy Frankfurt International Airport.
- China will account for 30 percent of global infrastructure spending over the next two decades. Your best bet is Emerging Global Shares China Infrastructure Index (ticker: CHXX).

CHAPTER SIX

Follow the Bouncing Ball

USING INTEREST RATE HEDGE TO

OFFSET MONETARY POLICY RISK

Nobody can predict interest rates.

—Peter Lynch, legendary investor

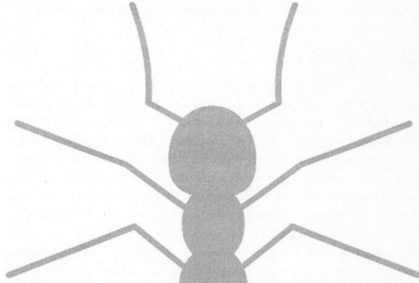

As an investor, it is always important to keep an eye on the ever-changing interest rate environment. Interest rates are at the core of capitalism. They determine the rate a borrower must pay for the use of the money from the lender.

Interest rates are either set by national governments or by central banks. Here in the United States our central bank is the Federal Reserve Board. They can set interest rates by moving the Federal Funds Rate higher or lower. Interest rates are the single most important tool for monetary policy, as the movement of interest rates up or down will have a dramatic impact on inflation and unemployment. Traditional investors in fixed incomes know that when interest rates rise their portfolio will fall. Meanwhile, savvy investors using ANTs will be able to watch their portfolio rise, when interest rates rise.

Why Do Rates Change?

Basically interest rates move as a result of one of three factors: monetary policy, inflation, or the supply and demand for money.

Monetary Policy

Think of monetary policy as the government's plan to move the economy faster or slower using interest rates. If a government loosens monetary policy, it simply means it is printing more money. Many people don't realize this; however, the central bank creates more money by simply printing it. This in turn makes interest rates move lower. The reason is because there is now more money available for lenders to lend and for borrowers to borrow, and that highly competitive landscape allows borrowers to shop around looking for lower rates.

On the other hand, if the supply of money is being lowered, meaning it is shrinking, on Wall Street we say monetary policy is tightening, and a tighter monetary policy causes interest rates to rise. When there is less money to lend, lenders can demand higher interest rates from potential borrowers. In this fashion central banks will alter the supply of money in order to move interest rates to manage the underlying economy.

Inflation

The second key driver of interest rates is inflation or, I should say, inflation expectations. Investors need to preserve the current "purchasing" power of their money. Here is how this works. If inflation is high and the expectation is that it could go even higher, investors will demand a higher interest rate if they are going to lend their money. Think about it like this. If you are a bond investor and inflation is only expected to be 2–3 percent over the next five years, a 5 percent bond is preserving your current purchasing power with a 2 percent cushion. As an investor, you are lending your money to the bond issuer for 5 percent and with inflation at 2–3 percent you are 2 percent ahead. This is a good investment.

Look what happens to that same investment if inflation dramatically shifts. You again lend your money for five years receiving 5 percent in return. But instead of tame inflation at 2–3 percent we have a case of hyperinflation at 8 percent. Now you are locked in for the next five years to receive 5 percent, and with inflation at 8 percent you are losing 3 percent of your current purchasing power each and every year.

Supply and Demand for Money

The third and final key driver of interest rates is the basic supply and demand for money. Remember interest rates are the price for borrowing money. So again, interest rates move up and down reflecting many different factors. Maybe no factor is more important than the supply of funds available for loans from lenders and the demand from borrowers. The best example of how this works is in the mortgage market. At a time when many people are borrowing money to buy houses, banks need to have money to lend. They can get that money from their own depositors. Banks can do that by paying 4 percent interest on a five-year certificate of deposit and then charge a borrower 6 percent interest on a five-year mortgage. If the demand for borrowing is higher than the funds they have available, they have to convince more depositors to give them more deposits. They do that by raising their certificate of deposit rates, which allows them, or forces them, to raise mortgage rates. The bottom line is that interest rates go up.

It is not just in banks that this occurs. It happens in the over-all bond market as well. If the economy is booming, many firms will want to borrow funds using the bond market to replace their inventory, expand their plants and facilities, or even to acquire other firms. At the same time corporations are borrowing money, and so are consumers to buy cars and houses. Governments are also borrowing more as they almost always spend more money than they collect in taxes. All of these things combined keep the demand for capital (funds) at a high level, which in turn keeps interest rates high.

Hedging Your Bets

Because the only thing that we know for sure is that interest rates are going to continue to move both up and down, it is important for investors, especially bond investors, to hedge that risk when interest rates begin to move. By hedging you are buying your-self some insurance. In the case of a bond market investor you are insuring yourself against a negative event like rising interest rates. It is important to remember that hedging does not prevent the nega-tive event from happening, but when it does happen, the impact of the event on your portfolio is reduced.

While I use the example of buying insurance to hedge in the world of investing, it isn't as simple as buying insurance as you do for your house, when you hedge against fires or other unforeseen natural disasters. As an investor, hedging against an investment risk means strategically using financial instruments in the market to off-set the risk of any adverse price movements, as in this case, when interest rates rise. In the world of investing, investors hedge one investment by simply making another investment. That is your insurance.

*Investors hedge one investment by simply
making another investment.*

Should I Float?

The best interest rate hedge is a floating rate security. These can either be floating rate bonds, bank loans, or other debt securities. Here is how they work. Most traditional bonds have fixed interest rates. This is why on Wall Street we call it the Fixed Income Market, while on Main Street it is called the Bond Market. The Fixed Income Market and the Bond Market are one and the same. Whether the traditional bond is issued by a corporation or a government—local, state, or federal—the interest rates are set when that bond is first issued. When I say fixed, I mean fixed. That interest rate does not and will not change for the entire life of the bond.

On the other side of the coin, we have a floating rate security. A floating rate security does not have a fixed interest rate. Instead it has a variable interest rate. Here is what it means to have a variable interest rate. The rates will vary, meaning they can go up or down. It is almost as though they are floating, hence the term floating rate securities. These interest rates float up or down to reflect changes in the current market and underlying economy.

When Does It Float?

You may be asking yourself, *When does it float?* Well, that depends on the particular floating rate security that you decide to invest in. These floating rate securities run the entire time frame spectrum. On some of them the interest rates change daily, and on others the rates change monthly, quarterly, or even annually. Some others have a specified precise interval when interest rates will be adjusted.

The interest rate is changed to keep it in sync with a predetermined interest rate benchmark. This benchmark interest rate is officially referred to as "the reference rate." Two of the most popular benchmarks that are used to set the interest rates on floating rate securities are the Federal Funds Rate, which I mentioned earlier in this chapter, and LIBOR (the London Interbank Offered Rate). The most common is LIBOR, which is the interest rate that creditworthy international banks dealing in eurodollars charge each other for large loans. This LIBOR rate globally is the base for other large eurodollar loans to less creditworthy corporations or governments. For example a politically unstable third world country may have to pay 2 percent over LIBOR when it borrows money.

How Does It Work?

Floating rate securities are a pretty simple concept to understand. Because of these variable interest rates, floating rate securities have a huge advantage over traditional fixed rate bonds. The reason is that their price will be less affected by changes in interest rates.

Let me go back to Bond Basics 101 to remind you how this works. If you own a fixed income bond, here is what changing interest rates will do to that investment.

When interest rates rise, the prices on all existing and outstanding bonds fall, and when interest rates fall, the prices on all existing and outstanding bonds rise. Just remember that things move in reverse. When rates go up, prices go down, and when rates go down, prices go up.

Here is why it works like that. When interest rates rise, let's say to 6 percent, the lower rates paid by older bonds of 5½ percent or lower are less attractive and because no one wants to buy them anymore their prices fall. After all, who would want a bond paying 5½ percent if they can get one that pays 6 percent?

It works the same in reverse. Let's flip that coin again and see how. When interest rates fall, let's say to 4 percent, prices for existing and outstanding bonds that are paying 5 percent or 5½ percent rise. The reason is that these bonds will pay a higher interest rate than the newly-issued ones. Who would buy a new 4 percent bond when they could own an existing 5 percent bond?

On the other hand, the interest rate on floating rate securities adjusts to reflect increases or decreases in the benchmark rate. When rates are falling, floating rate securities aren't very attractive; however, when interest rates are rising they just might be the best interest rate hedge there is.

They Act Differently

Because of this fundamental difference, floating rate securities behave differently from fixed rate securities that face the exact same market conditions. This sets the backdrop for a great way to diversify your investments. When interest rates rise, all of your fixed income investments will decline in value. However, if you also have exposure to floating rate investments, they will increase in value and, depending upon your asset allocation to this asset class, could more than make up for what you lost in fixed rate investments.

There is a price to pay. Floating rate securities do tend to have higher credit risk than traditional fixed rate securities. *Credit risk* means that the borrower may not be able to pay back the principal and interest in full. However, to compensate investors for that risk, floating rate securities offer higher yields. Also most floating rate securities are secured by collateral pledged by the borrower. That means in the unlikely event of a default on the loan, the collateral will be seized and liquidated to reimburse investors.

> *Because of this fundamental difference, floating rate securities behave differently from fixed rate securities that face the exact same market conditions.*

Funds Are Better

From an investment perspective, I believe the best way to get exposure to this asset class is in a mutual fund. The reason is that most floating rate securities are generally only available in large dollar amounts that make it very difficult for most individual investors to invest in. The second reason is diversification. By owning this asset class in a mutual fund, for the same dollar amount invested you are spreading your credit risk among multiple issuers instead of just one. When the credit risk is higher never put all of your eggs in one basket.

The S.S.F. (Senior, Secured, and Floating) Solution

If you think about it you don't need to protect or hedge your fixed income investments when interest rates go down, because the value of your investments goes up. You only need to hedge when interest rates go higher.

It is extremely important that you do so. A relatively small move in interest rates will lead to a much greater loss than one would think. Let's use 10-year Treasury bonds as an example. If the Federal Funds Rate (interest rate) rises 1 percent, a 10-year Treasury bond will lose 8.5 percent of its value. If the Federal Funds Rate moves 2 percent, it will cause a 17 percent drop in the price of a 10-year Treasury.

My solution is Senior Secured Floating-Rate Bonds. They are the best interest rate hedge you will find. The three most important attributes about these bonds are that they are senior, they are secured, and they are floating. Let's drill down a little on all three starting with senior.

Senior

Senior refers to the bondholder's position in the event of liquidation. *Senior* means very first in line, and it doesn't get any better than this. Senior debt takes priority over junior debt owed by the issuer. In the event that the issuer goes bankrupt, senior debt must be repaid before other creditors receive any payment.

Another way to look at this is that you are at the very top of the capital structure. From top to bottom the capital structure looks like this. First, senior debt, followed by junior debt, then subordinated debt, mezzanine debt, convertible debt, exchangeable debt, preferred equity, warrants, shareholder loans, and then common equity. No one in this entire capital structure gets one penny until the senior debt is paid in full. If you must be somewhere in the capital structure, you might as well be on top.

> *In the event that the issuer goes bankrupt, senior debt must be repaid before other creditors receive any payment.*

Secured

Secured means that this bond is secured or backed by a specific form of collateral. Examples of specific collateral are the company's buildings, equipment, and all inventories. It also always includes the right to any and all trademarks and patents. It always includes all of the company's cash as well as all of their accounts receivables.

Basically it means you as an investor are secured by everything they own. That is why in the unlikely event of a bankruptcy you stand to get more of your money back, in fact, almost twice as much. When a typical high yield bond goes into bankruptcy, investors on average get about 40 cents back. Senior secured bonds on the other hand get over 70 cents back.

Floating

The third and final attribute is floating. Again *floating* refers to the interest rate on the bonds. They simply reset or float every 30 to 90 days by a predetermined amount, called the spread, to reflect change in the benchmark interest rate, most likely LIBOR.

Watch how this works in a rising rate environment. Let's say that the benchmark LIBOR is 2 percent and the bond promises to pay 2 percent more than LIBOR; then the interest rate will initially be set at 4 percent (2 percent LIBOR + 2 percent spread = 4 percent). Ninety days later, if LIBOR increases to 3½ percent, the interest on the bond resets to 5½ percent (3.5 percent LIBOR + 2 percent spread = 5½ percent).

Let's compare that to a fixed interest rate bond initially paying 4 percent. It will never pay more than 4 percent regardless of how high interest rates climb.

Where to Invest

Your options are almost limitless in the mutual fund world. You can find open-ended mutual funds and a few closed-end funds. Some are called "floating rate," others are called "senior income," and many are classified as "loan participation funds."

You need to look for three things: it must be senior, secured, and floating. No other type of bond can offer the same preservation of capital and give you higher income when interest rates rise.

ANT Valorem

- The only thing that we know for sure is that interest rates are going to continue to move both up and down, which makes it critical for bond investors to hedge that risk when interest rates move.
- The best interest rate hedge is a floating rate security. These can either be floating rate bond funds, bank loans, or other debt securities.
- Remember "senior" refers to the bondholder position in the capital structure in the event of liquidation. "Senior" means "very first in line," and it doesn't get better than this.
- When you are "secured," your bond is backed and secured by a specific form of collateral that includes buildings, equipment, inventory, trademarks, patents, cash, and accounts receivables.
- "Floating" refers to the interest rate on the bonds. They simply reset or float every 30 to 90 days by a predetermined amount, called the spread, to reflect the change in the benchmark interest rate, most likely LIBOR.

CHAPTER SEVEN

Up, Up, and Away

USING INFLATION HEDGE TO PROTECT

YOUR PORTFOLIO

I continue to believe that the American people have a love-hate relationship with inflation. They hate inflation but love everything that causes it.

—William E. Simon, former
Secretary of the Treasury

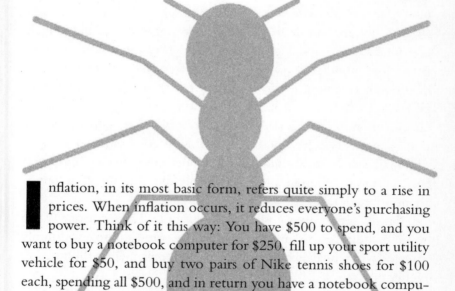

Inflation, in its most basic form, refers quite simply to a rise in prices. When inflation occurs, it reduces everyone's purchasing power. Think of it this way: You have $500 to spend, and you want to buy a notebook computer for $250, fill up your sport utility vehicle for $50, and buy two pairs of Nike tennis shoes for $100 each, spending all $500, and in return you have a notebook computer, two pairs of Nike tennis shoes, and a full tank of gas.

With inflation, let's say that the computer now costs $280, and your two pairs of Nike tennis shoes cost $110 each. You have already spent the same $500; however, this time you have no money left to fill that gas tank. In other words, the same amount of money has just bought you a smaller amount of goods and services. That is what a loss of purchasing power means: Spend the same amount of money and end up purchasing fewer goods. At least you have two pairs of Nike tennis shoes, which you need even more since you have no gas in your sports utility vehicle!

What Causes It?

Actually there are many different causes of inflation. Inflation can occur when governments print an excess of money to deal with an economic shock or a crisis. When there is more money in the system, prices always rise to keep up with all of that money. Think about it like this: With all of that money available, demand is high, and when demand is high, prices go higher, too. Another common cause of inflation is a rise in production costs. Any rise in production costs almost always leads to a rise in the price of the final product. Here is why it happens. Let's say the cost of raw materials, in this case cotton, rises dramatically in price. This means the cost of production just increased, so now it costs more to produce that same article of clothing. What happens next is that companies increase prices in order to continue to make a profit. The simple result is inflation.

Finally, rising labor costs almost always lead to inflation. When workers are able to demand more wages, most companies simply immediately pass that cost straight to the consumer in the form of higher prices.

Indexed for Inflation

From an investment perspective, one way to protect yourself from inflation is to invest in inflation-indexed bonds. In an inflation-indexed bond the principal amount of the bond is actually indexed to inflation. They are one of the best ways to reduce the inflation risk on your investment portfolio.

These inflation-indexed securities have been around for a long time. The Massachusetts Bay Company in 1780 issued the first ever inflation-indexed bond. In 1981 when the British government began issuing inflation-linked gilts, the market exploded. The term *gilt* is of British origin; it actually refers to the debt securities issued by the Bank of England, which had a gilt or gilded edge. That is why they are called "gilt-edged securities" or "gilts" for short. In 1997, the United States issued its first inflation-indexed bond called Treasury Inflation-Protected Securities or TIPS for short (more about these later). Today, the inflation-indexed market mostly consists of government bonds, with private-issued corporate inflation-indexed bonds comprising a very small portion of the market.

> *From an investment perspective, one way to protect yourself from inflation is to invest in inflation-indexed bonds.*

Global Trend

This trend toward investing in inflation-indexed bonds is now sweeping the globe. Currently, there are nine developed countries that offer these investments worldwide.

In addition to the previously-mentioned gilts from the United Kingdom, that link to inflation through that country's Retail Price Index (RPI), and Treasury Inflation-Protected Securities from the United States, that link to inflation through the U.S. Consumer Price Index (CPI), you have seven other global options.

Australia issues Capital Indexed Bonds (CAIN series) that link to inflation through the weighted average of eight capital cities called the All-Groups Index. In Canada, they issue a Real Return Bond (RRB) that is linked to inflation through the Canada All-Items CPI. France issues something called the OATi that is linked to inflation through the France CPI Ex-Tobacco Index. Germany issues its Bund index that links to inflation through the EU HICP Ex-Tobacco. (European Union–Harmonized Index of Consumer Prices). In Italy they issue BTPi that is linked to inflation by the very same EU HICP Ex-Tobacco. Japan issues JGBi that is linked to inflation through the Japan CPI Nationwide, Ex-Fresh Food. Finally we have Sweden that issues index-linked treasury bonds that are tied to inflation through the Swedish CPI.

TIPS

Let's dig a little deeper into these inflation-indexed bonds here in the United States called TIPS. "TIPS" stands for "Treasury Inflation-Protected Securities." They are inflation-indexed bonds issued by the U.S. Treasury. The principal on these bonds is adjusted to the Consumer Price Index, the most widely accepted measure of inflation in the United States.

The coupon rate is held constant, but it will generate different amounts of interest to the investor. This occurs when you multiply the coupon rate by the inflation-adjusted principal. It becomes a government guarantee that inflation will not eat into your investment. TIPS are currently offered in 5-year, 10-year, and 30-year maturities.

A Bond Is a Bond

These TIPS, at the end of the day, are still Treasury bonds. This is as good a time as ever for a quick refresher on Treasury bonds.

Treasury bonds have the longest maturity of all U.S. government securities: up to 30 years. They have a coupon payment every six months. The U.S. government suspended issuing the 30-year Treasury bond for a 4½-year period starting October 31, 2001, and concluding February 2006. These 30-year Treasury bonds are often simply referred to as long-bonds. When the U.S. government was aggressively using its budget surpluses to pay down its debt in the 1990s the 10-year Treasury note began to replace the 30-year Treasury bond as the general pulse of the U.S. bond market.

Because of demand from pension funds and large long-term institutional investors like university endowments as well as the need to diversify the Treasury Department's liabilities, the 30-year Treasury bond was re-introduced and is issued quarterly. This brought the United States back in sync with Europe and Japan by issuing longer-dated maturities.

Watch Inflation

Because the interest rate that you receive is dependent on what happens to inflation, any TIPS investor must have an understanding of inflation and how it is measured. The TIPS inflation link is the consumer price index (CPI) and that is where your focus needs to be.

The Consumer Price Index is a measure of the price level of consumer goods and services. The United States Bureau of Labor Statistics, which started this statistic in 1919, publishes the CPI on a monthly basis. It is actually calculated by measuring price changes among a wide array of products, weighing these changes in price against the share of income consumers spend purchasing them. The resulting statistic, measured as of the end of the month for which it is published, serves as one of the most popular and most widely followed measures of U.S. inflation.

You Need to Follow CPI-U

There is a subcomponent of the CPI Index that TIPS investors need to be aware of. It is called the CPI-U Index. The reason this is important is because TIPS are actually indexed against the Labor Department's CPI-U Index for all urban consumers. This all-urban consumer population consists of all urban households in Metropolitan Statistical Areas and in urban places of 2,500 inhabitants or more. Nonfarm consumers living in rural areas with Metropolitan Statistical Areas are also included, but the index excludes rural consumers and the military population. The Consumer Price Index for All Urban Consumers (CPI-U) was introduced in 1978.

Why TIPS?

As I travel all around the country, I am frequently asked by investors, "Why would I invest in TIPS, if there is no inflation?" I almost always answer with my favorite Donald Rumsfeld quote. Donald Rumsfeld was both the 13th and 21st United States Secretary of Defense. Here is what he said at a 2002 press briefing, "Reports that say that something hasn't happened are always interesting to me, because as we know, there are known knowns; these are things we know we know. We also know there are known unknowns; that is to say we know there are some things we do not know. But there are also unknown unknowns, the ones we don't know we don't know." The best example of that is when inflation arrives.

As an investor I would consider having an exposure to inflation-index bonds today because inflation will surely be here tomorrow, and here is why. The laws of economics and finance have not been repealed. The most basic law of all is this: If you print enough money to throw at a problem, you can solve that problem, and in its place you will have created a new problem—inflation.

Remember back to when the entire financial system appeared to be on the brink of collapse after Bear Stearns failed, followed by Lehman Brothers and AIG, and so on and so forth. Well, to save the financial world from complete collapse, virtually every country in the world pitched in. They either cut interest rates, or they cut personal taxes, or they cut business taxes. Many embarked on massive spending programs like China and the United States to get their economies moving again. Many more provided government guarantees to loans as well as directly bailing out companies or industries. Think General Motors here in the United States. When it was all said and done, it became the largest synchronized global monetary and fiscal policy response in the history of mankind. Because of this the world averted a financial meltdown, and the price we will pay for that is inflation.

Let me give you two other things to think about to show how I know inflation is coming. Forget all of the unprecedented government spending that has already occurred. I am more worried about what has to be spent in the future that will surely fuel inflation. Currently the United States has $110 trillion in unfunded liabilities for Social Security, Medicare, Medicaid, and the new universal health care benefits. At some point in time, we have to pay for all of this stuff! How do you spell "inflation"?

> *The most basic law of all is this: If you print enough money to throw at a problem, you can solve that problem, and in its place you will have created a new problem—inflation.*

The second reason is whenever we face the next economic hiccup I already know the response from most politicians: Let's throw a little more money at the problem and see if we can't get the economy moving again.

There is simply too much money chasing too few goods. When there is too much money chasing too few goods, the only answer is inflation.

Two TIPS Benefits

I like TIPS as my inflation-indexed bond because it gives me two great benefits over traditional inflation hedges like gold.

First and most important is the fact that I get regular interest payments. Remember: TIPS will pay you interest every six months just like a regular Treasury bond. The important distinction and benefit here is that unlike a traditional Treasury bond, TIPS principal actually increases each year by the amount of inflation as measured by the Consumer Price Index for urban consumers CPI-U. Your semiannual interest payments will also increase based on the amount of inflation.

The second reason I like TIPS is that it gives you a tax benefit as well. All TIPS interest that you receive is exempt from state and local income taxes, but just like traditional Treasury bonds, TIPS interest is taxable at the federal level.

> *Remember: TIPS will pay you interest every six months just like a regular Treasury bond.*

How to Buy

There are actually two very easy ways for an investor to get exposure to TIPS in their investment portfolio. First you can buy them directly from the U.S. Treasury Department over the Internet. Simply type in: www.treasurydirect.gov/indiv/research/indepth/tips/res_tips_buy.htm.

The second way to get TIPS exposure is through an exchange-traded fund. The best one is the iShares Barclays TIPS Bond Fund. Why is it the best? You will never forget its ticker on the New

York Stock Exchange—it is "TIP." This fund is actually designed to track Lehman Brothers' U.S. Treasury Inflation Notes Index that measures the performance of the inflation-protected public obligations of the U.S. Treasury, in other words, TIPS.

ANT Valorem

- In an inflation-indexed bond, the principal amount of the bond is actually linked to inflation, making it one of the best ways to reduce the inflation risk on your investment portfolio.
- Treasury Inflation-Protected Securities or TIPS are inflation-indexed bonds issued by the U.S. Treasury; the principal on these bonds is adjusted to the Consumer Price Index.
- There is simply too much money chasing too few goods. When there is too much money chasing too few goods the only answer is inflation.
- One way to invest in TIPS is to buy them directly from the U.S. Treasury Department at: www.treasurydirect.gov/indiv/research/indepth/tips/res_tips_buy.htm.
- You can also get TIPS exposure through an exchange-traded fund such as iShare Barclays TIPS Bond Fund, ticker "TIP."

CHAPTER EIGHT

"Derivatives" Isn't a Dirty Word

Using Derivatives to Reduce Risk

All living things are gnarly, in that they inevitably do things that are much more complex than one might have expected.
—Rudy Rucker, American mathematician,
computer scientist, science fiction author,
and philosopher

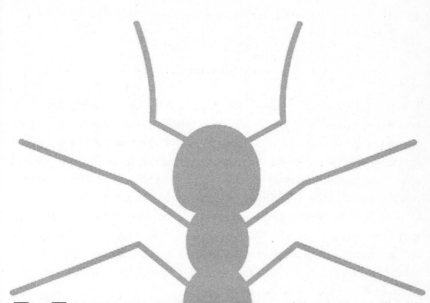

Most investors assume that the use of derivatives will add risk to any portfolio. *That is simply not true.* If used properly, derivatives will actually serve to *reduce* the overall risk in any portfolio which is why, in my opinion, all investors should be using some sort of a derivative in their portfolio.

Part of the problem is that a derivative is not an easy concept to explain because it has so many moving parts and it can be used in so many different ways. Here is the simplest way to think of a derivative. It is a financial instrument used by two parties that has a value that is determined by the actual price of something else. We call this "something else" the underlying asset. It's that underlying asset that has value and as a result can move up or down in price at any given time.

This is what causes so much of the confusion. The derivative itself is not an asset, because by itself it has no value. It is the underlying asset that has a price movement, and in turn an underlying value.

Types of Derivatives

Let me give you a broader perspective here before we jump into the details. Basically there are two types of derivatives. The two types are based upon the way these derivatives are actually traded in the market. There are exchange-traded derivative contracts and over-the-counter derivatives. Simply put, an exchange-traded derivative is a derivative instrument that is traded at a specialized derivative exchange. A derivative exchange is a market where individuals can buy and sell standardized contracts that have been created by the exchange. This derivative exchange acts as an intermediary on all related transactions and takes money from both parties on both sides of the trade as a guarantee.

The best example of a derivative exchange is right here in my hometown of Chicago: the CME Group, which was created in 2007 with the merger of the Chicago Mercantile Exchange and the Chicago Board of Trade. Then, in 2008, it acquired the New York Mercantile Exchange.

Conversely, over-the-counter derivatives are contracts that are privately negotiated and traded directly between the two parties without going through a derivatives exchange. This over-the-counter derivative market is the largest market for derivatives. It is, for the most part, unregulated especially with respect to disclosure information between parties. This market is made up primarily of banks, hedge funds, and high net worth individuals and sophisticated institutional investors like endowments and pension funds. Figuring out the exact size of this market is impossible because these trades and contracts occur in private and none of the activity is visible on any of the world's derivatives exchanges.

Uses of Derivatives

Just as there are two types of derivatives, there are basically only two general uses of a derivative. It can either be used as a hedge to reduce risk, or it can be used to speculate, which would add risk. Let's talk about hedging first, where we are actually attempting to reduce risk through the use of derivatives.

Used as a hedge, the derivative will allow the price movement of the underlying asset to be transferred from one party of the derivative contract to another. Think back to the section on commodities in Chapter 2 where I was discussing corn and suggested one possible way to invest in corn was to invest in Chevron because they are a leader in ethanol production that uses corn.

In my example, the corn farmer and Chevron could sign a futures contract to exchange a specific amount of corn for a specific amount of cash, at a specific date in the future. Many investors don't realize this, but by using this derivative hedging strategy both parties have actually reduced their risk in the future. Corn farmers will no longer have to worry about the uncertainty of the price they will be paid for their corn, and Chevron knows that they will have corn available to them exactly when they need it.

However, looked at another way, hedging does add an additional risk as well. Let's stick with my corn farmer and Chevron example. The corn farmer has taken on additional risk with this derivative contract because if the price of corn in the open market rises above the price in the contract, my corn farmer will lose all of that additional income. Even though this is an additional risk, it is somehow offset by looking at the other side of the coin. The corn farmer, by locking in a price, reduces the risk that the price of corn will fall below the price in the derivative contract.

> *Used as a hedge, the derivative will allow the price movement of the underlying asset to be transferred from one party of the derivative contract to another.*

The same can be said for the other party in my example. Chevron is taking on the risk that the price of corn in the open market will fall below the price in the derivative contract, meaning Chevron will actually have to pay a higher price for their corn. But again there are two sides to this as well. Chevron has reduced the risk that the price of corn will rise above the amount set forth in the derivative contract.

The other use of derivatives, for speculation, is always about acquiring and taking on additional risk and is never used to reduce risk.

Both individual investors as well as institutional investors will enter into a derivative contract so that they can speculate on the value of the underlying asset whatever that may be. They are actually placing a bet that the other party to the contract will be wrong about what the future value of the underlying asset will be.

This is classic buy low and sell high only using derivatives to define the actual time frame. Look at it this way: A speculator wants to be able to buy the underlying asset in the future at the low price already established in the derivative contract in the hope that when the time comes to buy it the actual market price will be much higher. Everything between the low derivative contract price and the higher actual market price will be all pure profit to the speculator.

It works the other way as well. A speculator may want to sell the underlying asset in the future at a high price according to the derivative contract in the hope that when the time comes to sell it the actual market price will be much lower. Again everything between the high derivative contract price and the lower actual market price will be all pure profit to the speculator.

Classifications of Derivatives Contracts

There are four basic classifications of derivatives contracts. First there is a "futures" contract, which is a contract to buy or to sell an asset at a future date with the price being agreed to in the contract today. All futures contracts are standardized contracts written by a clearing house that operates an exchange (think C.M.E. Group) where the contract can be bought and sold.

The second classification of a derivatives contract, a "forward" contract, is very similar to a futures contract in that it is a contract to buy or sell an asset at a future date with the price being agreed to in the contract today. The difference is the forward contract is not a standardized contract and is written by the parties themselves.

Third we have "options" contracts. These are contracts that give the owner the right, but not the obligation, to buy or to sell an underlying asset, depending on the specific type of option. The price at which the sale takes place is known as the strike price and is specified at the time the parties enter into the contract. The options contract has an end date known as its maturity date.

Fourth and finally is a "swaps" contract. This is a contract to exchange cash on or before a specified future date based on the value of some underlying asset like a currency, a bond, a commodity, a stock, or some other investable asset. Let's take a closer look at all four of these classifications beginning with the futures contract.

Futures Contract

Again, a futures contract is a standardized contract between two parties to buy or sell a specified underlying asset at a specified future date at an agreed upon price today. The contracts are traded on a futures exchange like the C.M.E. Group.

The party agreeing to buy the underlying asset in the future is assuming what we refer to on Wall Street as a "long" position. Conversely, the party agreeing to sell the asset in the future assumes a "short" position.

Here is an important distinction about futures contracts. They are not direct securities like stocks or bonds. Instead they are an indirect security based on the underlying asset in the derivative contract.

The actual underlying assets to a futures contract are not limited to the traditional assets of stocks and bonds. The futures contract could have as its underlying asset a currency or a commodity or even interest rates.

The Future Is Now

The actual future date that is identified in the derivative contract is the delivery date. It can also be referred to as the final settlement date. These terms are one and the same and are used interchangeably. The settlement price is the price of the futures contract at the end of a day's trading session for that day of trading on the exchange. Thus, everyday you will know the exact value of your futures contract.

When you enter into a futures contract, your strategy has just been written in stone. That is because a futures contract gives you an obligation to buy or to sell an underlying asset based on the terms of the derivative contract. It is not an option of something you may want to do, but rather something you must do. Both parties of a futures contract by law must fulfill the terms of the contract on the actual settlement date. The seller is required to deliver the underlying asset to the buyer. If it is a cash-settled futures contract, then the actual cash is transferred from the futures trader who lost money to the futures trader who made money on the contract.

Remember, a futures contract is an exchange-traded derivative. The exchange's clearinghouse acts as counterparty on all contracts and, as such, sets margin requirements, provides a mechanism for settlement, and sets forth the standard guidelines for all contracts. Let's take a look at all three of these aspects, beginning with margin.

Margin

In order to minimize the financial risk to the exchange, traders must post a margin. Think of it as a down payment, so to speak. The amount of this margin (down payment) typically ranges between 5 percent and 15 percent of the overall value of the contract.

Now, in order to minimize the counterparty's risk to traders (that is the risk that the trader at the other end of the contract, i.e., counterparty will not live up to their end of the contract), all trades executed on regulated futures exchanges are guaranteed by a clearinghouse. Here is the best way to think of a clearinghouse. If needed, it will be the buyer to every seller and the seller to every buyer in the event the counterparty (the other trader to the futures contract defaults and can't live up to their end of the deal). Without these provisions, it would take forever to agree to any contract because all traders would be required to do extensive due diligence on every trader they were thinking of doing a futures contract with to make sure that there was no counterparty risk.

The initial margin is the amount of equity (cash) required to establish the futures contract. It is very important for investors to realize that the maximum amount of equity or cash is not limited to the amount of the initial margin. In the event of a loss, the value of the initial margin will be eroded, and in that case the broker will make a margin call in order to restore things back to the amount of the initial margin level.

This is often referred to as "variation" margin, so named because these margin calls are usually made on a daily basis; however, in times of extreme price movements a broker can make a margin call intraday. All calls for margin must be paid and received on the day they are made. If not, the broker has the discretion to close out any positions necessary to meet these margin requirements, and the client is responsible to pay up for any losses or deficits that these actions may have caused.

Here is a very simple way to think of it. All futures contracts and accounts are marked to market (priced) daily. If the margin drops below the margin maintenance requirement established by the exchange listing the futures, a margin call will be issued to bring the account back up to the required level.

Settlement

Let's move on to our second aspect, settlement. Simply put, settlement is how you are going to live up to the terms of the contract and settle up. There are only two settlement options: physical delivery or cash settlement.

Physical delivery is when the actual amount specified of the underlying asset of the futures contract is delivered by the seller of the contract to the exchange, so that in turn the exchange can then deliver it to the buyer of the contract. This form of delivery is most often used with bonds and commodities. In the real world, this type of settlement is only used in a tiny minority of contracts. Instead most contracts are simply cancelled out by purchasing a covering position, which is buying a contract to cancel out an earlier sale or selling a contract to liquidate an earlier purchase.

Meanwhile, cash settlement is when a cash payment is made based on the underlying reference value such as a stock market index. The traders to the futures contract settle by paying (or by receiving) the loss (or receiving the gain) related to the contract in cash when the futures contract expires.

Contract Components

Let's move on to our third and final aspect, which is the contract itself. Almost all futures contracts contain the same six elements to ensure their liquidity by being very standardized. The six components are first, clearly identifying the underlying asset, which could be anything from a stock market index to gold. Second, it identifies the exact number of units of the underlying asset per futures contract, such as 10 ounces of gold. Third, all contracts identify the delivery month. Fourth, they identify the last trading date. Fifth, they identify the type of settlement: cash or physical. Sixth and finally, they reference the currency in which the futures contract is quoted in. Because most contracts have these six components, this standardization creates a very liquid market.

History

Let me end where it all began, by giving you a little historical perspective of futures contracts. It is believed that the first futures exchange market was in Japan in the 1700s. It was called the Dojima Rice Exchange and was created to meet the needs of a samurai who was being paid in, you guessed it, rice. After a series of bad rice harvests he needed to have a more stable option to convert his rice into a usable currency.

This will surely confuse you. The Chicago Board of Trade listed the first-ever standardized exchange-traded "forward contracts" in 1864, which were called "futures contracts." This first contract was on grain trading and began the global expansion of a vast number of commodities all around the globe. Talk about quickly going global. Within 10 years, cotton futures were being traded halfway around the world from Chicago to Mumbai, India, and the rest is history.

> *The first futures exchange market was in Japan in the 1700s. It was called the Dojima Rice Exchange and was created to meet the needs of a samurai who was being paid in, you guessed it, rice.*

Forward Contract

Let's move on to our second of four derivatives contracts classifications, forwards. As you have probably guessed by now, a forward contract is a nonstandardized contract between two parties to buy or sell an asset at a specified future time at a price agreed upon today. As an investor, it will cost you nothing to enter into a forward contract. The party agreeing to buy the underlying asset in the future assumes what Wall Street refers to as the "long" position, and the party agreeing to sell the asset in the future assumes the "short" position. This is what it means if you have ever heard someone say they were long or short a particular stock. Now the price agreed upon is called the delivery price.

Spot Price

The forward price of such a contract is commonly contrasted to the spot price, which is the actual price at which the asset changes hands on the spot date. So the difference between the spot and the forward price is what Wall Street calls the "forward premium" or "forward discount." In other words it is the profit or loss by the purchasing party.

Not a Future

In many respects this may seem like a futures contract, but it isn't. Forward contracts are not exchange traded and they are not standardized. Also, forwards have no interim or partial settlements in their margin requirements like futures do. So what that means is with a forward the parties do not exchange additional equity (or cash) whenever there is a daily loss or gain. Instead they let it all ride. The entire unrealized gain or loss continues to build until the forward contract is settled.

Golden Example

Here is a great example of how a forward contract works. Let's say that my wife, Cheryl, wanted to buy gold a year from now because she is worried about all of the geopolitical risk in this country. Now let's just say at the same time Ben Bernanke currently owns some gold valued at $250,000 that he wants to sell a year from now as he is convinced we will have a Goldilocks recovery here in the United States and everything will be just fine. My wife Cheryl and Ben Bernanke could enter into a forward contract with each other. Suppose they both agree on the sale price of Ben's gold (which is currently valued at $250,000) in one year's time of $275,000. This is quite simply all a forward contract is. My wife Cheryl and Ben Bernanke have a forward contractual agreement. Now because she is buying the underlying asset (gold), my wife, Cheryl, is said to have entered into a "long" forward contract. Conversely, Ben Bernanke will have the "short" forward contract.

So let's fast-forward one year to where the current market value of Ben Bernanke's gold is $315,000. But, because Ben is obligated to sell it to my wife Cheryl for only $275,000, she just made a $40,000 profit. Here is why. Cheryl gets to buy the gold from Ben Bernanke today for $275,000 and then immediately sell it at the current market price of $315,000. Cheryl has made the difference ($40,000) in profit. Ben Bernanke, on the other hand, has a potential loss of $40,000, and an actual profit of $25,000 (gold was worth $250,000 when he entered the forward contract, and now he is getting paid $275,000 which is a $25,000 profit).

Options Contract

Let's move on to the third classification of derivative contracts, options. An options contract is a legal financial instrument between two parties regarding the buying or the selling of an asset at a specified price during a specified time frame. Under an options contract, the buyer gains the "option" or the legal right, but not the obligation, to engage in some specific transaction (buy or sell) on the underlying asset. It is important to note that you have the right but not the obligation to engage in some specific transaction. Meanwhile the seller does incur the obligation and must do so if requested by the buyer.

The actual price of an option depends on the value of the underlying asset (most likely a stock or bond) plus a premium based on the time remaining until the option expires.

In the broadest of terms, an option that gives you the right to buy something is referred to on Wall Street as a "call." On the other side of the coin, Wall Street calls an option that gives the right to sell a "put." The actual price that is specified when the underlying asset may be traded is called the "strike price." When people exercise their option, they are simply trading the underlying asset at the agreed-upon price. All options have an expiration date attached to them. If the option is not exercised by the expiration date, it becomes void and can no longer be exercised.

You might be asking yourself why anyone would grant someone an option. That's easy, for the money. In return for granting the option, you collect a payment, which is a premium, from the buyer. An investor who grants an option must make good on delivering the underlying asset if the option is exercised.

> *Under an options contract, the buyer gains the "option" or the legal right, but not the obligation, to engage in some specific transaction (buy or sell) on the underlying asset.*

A Matter of Style

There are six general styles of options. First, there is an "American option," which is an option that can be exercised on any trading day on or before it expires. Second, there is a "barrier option," which is an option that has a specific characteristic that the underlying asset price must first pass through a certain minimum level (a barrier if you will) before it can be exercised. Third, there is a "Bermudan option," which is an option that may be exercised only on specified dates on or before the expiration date. Fourth is the "European option," which is an option that may only be exercised at expiration. Fifth, there are "exotic options," which are options that include complex structures and terms. Sixth and finally is the "vanilla option," which basically is anything that isn't exotic—think plain vanilla. Let's see exactly how this works using the American style. An option in the U.S. markets typically represents 100 shares of the underlying asset. There are four basic trades to be made with an option. Let's look at all four.

Long Call

First there is the "long call." An investor who thinks that a stock's price will increase could buy the right to purchase the stock, a call option, rather than just buy the stock itself. An investor would do that because for the same amount of money an investor can control a much larger number of shares. In other words the investor is leveraging the investment.

An investor would have no obligation to buy the stock, only the option or right to do so until the expiration date. Here is how it works. If the underlying asset's stock price at expiration is above the agreed-upon exercise price by more than the premium or the cost of the long call, the investor will profit. However, if the underlying asset stock price at expiration is lower than the agreed-upon exercise price, the investor will simply let the long call contract expire and will only lose the amount of money paid, or the premium.

Long Put

Second there is a "long put." An investor who thinks that a stock's price will decrease can buy the option or right to sell the stock at a fixed price which is a put option. The investor has no obligation to sell the stock, but rather the option or right to do so until the expiration.

It would work like this. If the underlying asset's stock price at expiration is below the exercise price by more than the amount of the premium paid, that investor will profit. If, however, the underlying asset stock price at expiration is above the exercise price, the investor will instead let this long put expire worthless and only lose the premium that they paid.

Short Call

Third we have a "short call." This would be used by an investor who thinks that a stock price will decrease and will write or sell a short call. The investor selling the short call has an absolute obligation to sell the stock to the short call buyer at the buyer's option. Here is how it works. If the underlying asset's stock price decreases, this short call position will make a profit in the amount of the premium paid. On the other hand, if the underlying asset's stock price increases over the exercise price by more than the amount of the premium, the short call writer will lose money, and the potential loss is unlimited as stock prices in theory could go to the moon.

Short Put

Fourth and finally is a "short put." This is used by an investor who believes that the underlying assets stock will increase, so the investor sells a put. The investor who sells a put has an obligation to buy the stock from the put buyer at the put buyer's option.

It would work like this. If the underlying asset's stock price at the expiration date is above the exercise price, the short put position will make a profit equal to the amount of the premium paid. However, if the stock price at expiration is below the exercise price by more than the cost or the price of the premium, the investor will lose money; however, the loss is capped at the full value of the stock price as a stock cannot go below zero.

Swap Contract

Time to move on to the fourth and final classification of derivative contracts, a swap contract. In a swap contract, investors exchange (or swap) certain provisions of one financial instrument for those in the other investor's financial instrument. The benefit to this contract depends on the financial instruments involved. Specifically, the two investors agree to exchange one stream of cash flows against another. Wall Street refers to these streams as the "legs" of the swap. The swap contract defines the dates when the cash flows are to be paid and on how to calculate the cash flow.

When the swap contract is initiated, at least one of these legs of cash flow is determined by a random or uncertain variable like interest rates, stock prices, or foreign currency exchange rates. Swap contracts are relatively new as the first ones were negotiated by Salomon Brothers in the early 1980s.

High Five

There are five basic types of swaps.

1. An interest rate swap, where you exchange a fixed rate loan for a floating rate loan or vice versa.
2. Currency swaps, where you exchange the principal and interest payments of a loan in one currency for the principal and interest rates of a loan in another currency.
3. A commodity swap, where a floating price is exchanged for a fixed price. This is almost always done using crude oil.
4. An equity swap, where you have an underlying asset as one stock, a number of stocks, or even a stock index.
5. Credit default swaps, contracts where the buyer makes a series of payments to the seller and receives a payoff if the credit instrument goes into default.

🐜 ANT Valorem

- Remember: There are basically only two general uses of a derivative. It can either be used as a hedge to reduce risk, or it can be used to speculate, which would add risk.
- "Futures" contracts are contracts to buy or sell an asset at a future date with the price being agreed today. All futures contracts are bought and sold on an exchange.
- "Forward" contracts do the same thing as futures contracts, except that they are not standardized and they are not sold on an exchange; instead the transaction is only between those two parties.
- "Options" contracts give the owner the right but not the obligation to buy or sell at a future date at a strike price agreed upon today.
- "Swaps" contracts exchange cash based on the value of an underlying asset like a currency or a stock.

CHAPTER NINE

Garage Sale Anyone?

INVESTING IN COLLECTIBLES

Quickly, bring me a beaker of wine, so that I may wet my mind and say something clever.

—Aristophanes

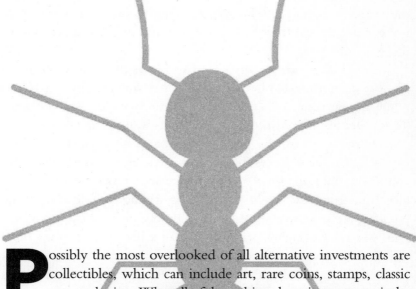

Possibly the most overlooked of all alternative investments are collectibles, which can include art, rare coins, stamps, classic cars, and wine. What all of these things have in common is the potential to appreciate in value. Collectibles are unique in that they do not generate any type of cash flow while you own them. Instead, they provide you with exposure to an asset class with very low correlation to the overall market. This in turn will actually lower the risk of your portfolio; plus, they are tangible. You can touch them, feel them, use them, and enjoy them while you are investing in them.

First, Collect Your Thoughts

Before you jump in with both feet and decide to invest in collectibles, here are four things that you need to think about.

133

First, take the time to gain some knowledge about the collectibles in which you are thinking of investing. You need to be able to determine the value of the specific collectible that you are looking to invest in. The biggest mistake that investors make is that they pay too much for a collectible because they don't have the expertise required to judge the value of a particular item. Here is a general rule of thumb: If you know nothing about art, do not invest in art!

Second, there are no current price lists as there are with stocks and bonds and most other alternative investments. If you pay too much or sell your collectible for too little, you have no recourse. That is because the market for collectibles is unregulated.

Third, this is not the place to make a quick buck. Collectibles can be a long, slow process before you make any money at all. There is basically only one time you will make your money with collectibles. You first must buy it and then be willing to hold it until the price appreciates in value. When you do decide to sell your collectible, you want a higher price for it than when you bought it, and this could take years to accomplish.

Fourth and finally, collectibles are illiquid assets. That means they are not easily or readily converted into cash.

Now that we have a better understanding of the basic characteristics of collectible investing, let's explore the major categories of collection: art, rare coins, stamps, classic cars, and wine.

Art

So the most basic question here is *Do you want to look at and enjoy your investment in art or do you simply want to make money in art?* If you want to enjoy your investment, then you need to head down the path of purchasing individual pieces of art. Heading down this path, most investors are almost always conflicted by the art they like as opposed to the art that has the greatest chance to appreciate in value.

Mei Moses Fine Art Index

Believe it or not, if you don't want to invest in one painting at a time you can first follow the overall art market. Two New York University Stern School of Business professors, Jiangping Mei and Michael Moses, have been compiling data that allows them to track the long-term performance of fine art. The result is the Mei Moses Fine Art Index. The index focuses on mature artists whose works command significant prices at auction. The index takes the original sale price and then subtracts it from the most recent sale price to calculate an annual return for a single painting.

Art Funds

There have been several art funds that have been launched over the years. In 2007, Société Générale Asset Management promoted a Luxembourg Alternative Investment Art Fund.

There is the Competitor Fine Art Fund (FAF) based in London established by former Christie's chief financial officer, Philip Hoffman. It focuses on "blue chip" art: Most works in its portfolio value between $500,000 and $2 million.

The China Fund, which was founded by former Sotheby's executive Julian Thompson, specializes in Asian art especially Chinese ceramics. There is a Russian fund called Aurora managed by Vladimir Voronchenko.

A hedge fund was launched in 2007 as a Guernsey-listed closed-end company called the Art Trading Fund. It is managed by Chris Carlson's Artistic Investment Advisors.

My favorite is the Sharpe Art Fund. The fund invests in European, U.S., Asian, and African art. It spreads its art investment among all art forms, which is why I like this fund. In this fund you will find investments in paintings, drawings, photos, graphics, and sculptures. To invest in the fund, go to their web site, www.sharpeartfund.com.

Rare Coins

Let's now move on to our second category of collectibles, rare coins. The main thing that makes a particular coin valuable is supply and demand. Lots of demand for a coin will cause its price to rise. That alone does not make it rare. Most coins are either in silver or gold. These investments should be considered a long-term investment with a time horizon of 10 years.

Silver Coins

The best silver coin investment is the Canadian Silver Maple Leaf and is 99.99 percent pure silver. Investors consider this coin fine silver. Actually there are two classifications: fine silver and junk silver. Junk silver is referring to older coins which a have much smaller percentage of silver in them.

For example, all U.S. coins dated 1964 and older including half dollars, quarters, and dimes are 90 percent silver. Junk silver coins are also available as sterling silver coins, which were minted in the United Kingdom and Canada until 1919. Australia continued to produce these sterling silver coins until 1945. All of these coins are 92.5 percent silver and can be found in denominations of crowns, half-crowns, florins, shillings, sixpence, and threepence. In addition, from 1920 to 1967 Canada produced coins with 80 percent silver content.

> *The best silver coin investment is the Canadian Silver Maple Leaf and is 99.99 percent pure silver.*

Gold Coins

Shifting gears from silver to gold, investors have two basic choices when looking to make an investment in gold coins. First, you could invest in gold bullion coins, which are issued every year by many countries. Investors have a very easy and very affordable way to get exposure to gold coins. It is affordable because these gold bullion coins sell for a small premium over the current spot price of gold. You can choose from the American Gold Eagle, Canadian Gold Maple Leaf, South African Kruggerand, or the Chinese Panda.

Your second choice would be to invest in numismatic (collector's items) golden coins. These coins were issued in great volumes in their day when the common currency was coins made of precious metal like gold. When investing in these coins, you will be paying a very large premium over the current spot price of gold. Your choices of numismatic gold coins include American Indian Heads, Liberty Caps, St. Gaudens, or Double Eagles. On the other side of the pond in Europe you can choose from European ducats or crowns, to get your gold coin exposure.

Stamps

Our third category of collectibles is stamps. It is very difficult, if not impossible, to get a handle on the size of this market. That is because the majority of these transactions in the buying and selling of stamps take place informally by mail. There is also a great deal of business done in retail establishments all over the globe.

The current estimate compiled by *Stamp Magazine* in the United Kingdom estimates there are 48 million stamp collectors worldwide including 18 million in China.

The current estimate compiled by Stamp Magazine *in the United Kingdom estimates there are 48 million stamp collectors worldwide including 18 million in China.*

SG100 Stamp Index

Believe it or not you can actually track the overall performance of stamp investing. Beginning in 2002 Stanley Gibbons compiled the SG100 Stamp Index based on both retail and auction prices for the "top 100 most frequently traded stamps" in the world.

Why Invest in Stamps

An investment in stamps would provide an investor some very interesting benefits that most investors don't think about. Here are three that come to mind. First, there is a finite supply of rare and classic stamps, meaning supply stays constant. Second, there are millions upon millions of stamp collectors around the world, creating a global marketplace for stamps, and this base continues to grow, meaning so does potential demand. Third, stamps are the most portable of all collectible investments. You can take your wealth with you wherever you go.

One final thing to think about: Don't forget the baby boomers. The baby boomers, the largest demographic cohort in the entire history of the United States, are heading toward retirement. What happens if in their retirement these 76 million boomers decide to resume their childhood hobby of stamp collecting? I speak from firsthand experience here: Even though I was not a stamp collector in my youth, my baby boomer wife, Cheryl, had a huge stamp collection passed down to her from her father.

Classic Cars

The fourth category of collectibles is classic cars. As with any collectible, there is more than just the age of the vehicle that makes it a classic. The age of the vehicle does play a factor; however, the more important issue is what is the particular make and model.

Don't be misled by the insurance industry. Most insurance agencies regard a classic car as anything over 15 years old. There are vast numbers of 15-year-old cars that will never be classics. The goal here is to find a car in limited quantity that everyone wants to own, which is what makes a classic. Classic cars have a certain mystique to them that few if any other investments have.

Follow the Numbers

The most important piece of advice I can give you regarding investing in classic cars is to follow the numbers; they will tell you everything.

The number I am talking about is the vehicle identification number, which is commonly referred to as the VIN. It is typically a series of 13 or 14 digits with a random letter thrown in. While the VIN for different manufacturers will tell you slightly different things, in general here is what that number can tell you. The first digit represents the manufacturer of the car: "4" is for Chevrolet and "5" is for Ford. The next two digits typically tell the engine type, the digits "57" could denote an 8-cylinder. The next two digits denote the body style of the car, "49" being a two-door convertible coup. The next two numbers denote the year of the car; "66" means 1966. The random letter stands for the facility at which the car was manufactured. For example a "P" would stand for Pittsburgh. The final 5 or 6 numbers denote that this was the 105,216th car that Chevrolet or Ford produced that day.

Before you buy a classic car do your homework and make sure you know exactly what the VIN on the car you are buying is telling you.

Wine

You guessed it; I saved the best category for last, wine. If your investment doesn't work out, you can always just sit back and drown your sorrows in a lovely glass of wine! Besides being able to drink your wine, there are financial incentives to buying wine.

Overall Market

Once again, this time with wine, there has been an index that has been created, so that as an investor you can track the performance of the overall wine market. The London International Vintners Exchange, Liv-Ex, is an electronic trading platform for fine wine. It was launched in 2000 and tracks the price of 100 wines. It is officially called the Liv-Ex 100. You can follow it by going to their web site www.liv-ex.com.

Four to Look Out For

As an investor, if you are thinking of making an investment in wine, there are four aspects that you need to pay close attention to if you want to be successful.

First, where is the wine from? The provenance and region where the wine is produced is a key to the ultimate value of the wine. If you want a safe bet, stick with only the best regions like Bordeaux or Champagne.

Second, if you are doing this as an investment, you need to know the shelf life of the wine. Actually the longevity of the wine is determined by the grape itself. Red wine made from Cabernet Sauvignons and Syrahs are the best for long-term aging and investing. White wine made from the Chenin Blanc grape have the best white longevity. Rosé wine is the worst and has no longevity.

Third, look at its price history. This is easy to do by looking at the Liv-Ex 100 Index. Historically, price appreciation favors the Bordeaux and Lafite regions.

Fourth and finally, figure out where you are going to sell your wine and to whom in order to make a profit. In the age of the Internet, this process just got a whole lot easier. There is online wine trading where you can buy and sell wine through VWF Trading. Simply log onto their web site at www.vwftrading.com and you are ready to sell or buy.

> *The longevity of the wine is determined by the grape itself.*

Wine Fund

One final way to invest in wine in Europe is through a wine fund, which is similar in principal to a mutual fund. The best one is the Vintage Wine Fund (www.vintagewinefund.com). The Vintage Wine Fund is a Cayman-based investment company, which was established to invest in fine wine with an objective of steady high capital growth.

The fund is managed by OWC Asset Management Limited, a London based wine investment company and is regulated by the Financial Services Authority (FSA). The fund invests in top wines from many different regions. Currently the fund is investing in wines from Bordeaux, Burgundy, Tuscany, Piedmont, Champagne, Spain, Portugal, California, and Australia.

ANT Valorem

- Remember, if you pay too much or sell your collectible for too little, you have no recourse, because the market for collectibles is unregulated.
- The best way to invest in art is with the Sharpe Art Fund, which invests in all art forms (www.sharpeartfund.com).
- When investing in numismatic (collectors' items) gold coins, you will be paying a very large premium over the current spot price of gold.
- Stamps are the most portable of all collectible investments. You can take your wealth with you wherever you go.
- A great way to invest in wine is through the Vintage Wine Fund (www.vintagewinefund.com), which invests in fine wine from many different regions.

PART TWO

Advice for ANTs

CHAPTER TEN

ANTs Go Marching Two by Two

Hiring a Financial Adviser

A goal, without a plan, is just a wish.
—Antoine de Saint Exupéry

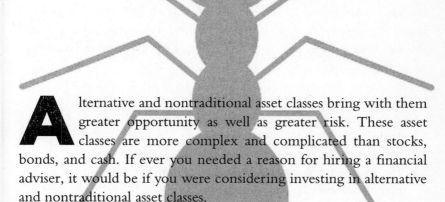

Alternative and nontraditional asset classes bring with them greater opportunity as well as greater risk. These asset classes are more complex and complicated than stocks, bonds, and cash. If ever you needed a reason for hiring a financial adviser, it would be if you were considering investing in alternative and nontraditional asset classes.

Yet one of the biggest mistakes individual investors continue to make is the temptation to go it alone without a financial adviser. The reason why many investors still do this is that there appears to be no cost with this option. That is a big mistake. While on the surface it may appear that you are saving money, in the long run this decision may cost you dearly.

Why Do You Need One?

Before you begin the process of hiring a financial adviser, you first must have a clear understanding of why you need one. There are right reasons and wrong reasons to hire a financial adviser.

Let me start with the wrong reason and quite sadly the reason many investors hire a financial adviser. They want to beat the market! Don't be fooled into picking a financial adviser who talks about his great stock-picking ability and his ability to beat the market. Advisers who tend to outperform and beat the market with their great stock picks one year, usually underperform the next year. No one can beat the market in the long run. You shouldn't be looking for a financial adviser that is smarter than the market, because none exists. Conversely if a financial adviser tells you he is smarter than the market or can beat the market, my advice is run the other way. So if you are not supposed to hire a financial adviser to beat the market why do you need one?

I believe there are three fundamental reasons to hire a financial adviser:

1. He offers objective advice.
2. He can guide you in making complex investments.
3. He can assist you in developing a plan or putting all of the pieces together.

There is no doubt in my mind that every investor would be better off with a financial adviser because that financial adviser can offer objective advice.

Why is objective advice important? It is because investing is an extremely emotional experience and emotions are what lead most investors to make the wrong decisions. When you invest emotionally, you tend to act impulsively or even irrationally. An adviser will help remove the emotion of investing by providing you objective and unemotional advice. Sometimes the best advice from advisers is when they get you to do nothing instead of doing what your emotions are telling you to do. When your emotions are driving investment decisions, investors will buy high and sell low. With the objective advice of a financial adviser, you will greatly increase your chances to buy low and sell high.

The second reason you should hire a financial adviser is if you are investing beyond the traditional big three asset classes of stocks, bonds, and cash. Alternative and nontraditional asset classes are very complex and complicated investment instruments. Advisers can add their expertise to help you understand the risk and opportunity of alternative and nontraditional assets.

The third and final reason is that a financial adviser will help you develop a plan. Think of this plan as putting all the pieces together for you. Even if as an individual investor you have the knowledge, time, and interest to do your investments on your own, no one can also have the time, interest, and know-how to handle their taxes and the time, interest, and know-how to develop a long-term financial plan. I have yet to meet individual investors who can do it all on their own. No one alone can fully understand all of the interactions among investing, taxes, and financial planning. Most people who try to do it alone will more often than not make a bad decision because they won't have the help of a financial adviser who knows and understands how all of the moving parts work.

How to Choose

When choosing financial advisers, I would say that maybe the single most important trait is that they need to be a good listener.

They need to listen to you so that they can identify your goals and needs and concerns and make sure that these are included in your financial plan. A good financial adviser will be able to quickly apply the right investment solutions to your goals, needs, and concerns.

The second attribute to look for in a financial adviser is his ability to not hesitate to encourage you and recommend that you engage other professionals to fill in where his expertise ends. You will never find a financial adviser who has expertise in investing, financial planning, accounting and tax matters, and law and legal issues. Your financial adviser is the one that should suggest or recommend that you update a will or place your investments in a trust. However, you need an attorney to actually draft the documents and possibly make even more informed suggestions. Likewise a good financial adviser will always have an eye on the tax ramifications of any investment strategy. That doesn't mean that you shouldn't still have a professional accountant or tax adviser prepare your taxes and work with you and your financial adviser.

So assuming you can find a few financial advisers who are good listeners and ones who are not hesitant to engage other professionals, how do you choose among them? I would suggest you begin by looking at three things: credentials, references, and fees.

Evaluating an Adviser's Credentials

You must put in the time to check your financial adviser's credentials. Every financial adviser must be registered in compliance with regulatory requirements. A financial adviser who is charging a fee and offering investment advice is required to be registered with the Securities and Exchange Commission and also by the state in which you live. Financial advisers dealing with insurance must hold insurance licenses granted by the appropriate insurance authorities, usually at the state level.

Most individual investors are shocked to find out that despite the requirement for licenses and registrations the financial adviser business is not what you would call highly regulated. Financial advising is still one of the fastest-growing professions. The barriers to entry are quite low. If you have enough money to pay the registrations fees and have a cell phone, you are in business!

I have met thousands upon thousands of financial advisers in my over-30-year career. Most, if not all, are highly ethical, sincere, honest, and hardworking. That is not enough. I would consider these traits as a given. You need a financial adviser who knows the business inside and out and upside down as well. You must find a financial adviser who will translate your goals and dreams and concerns into a realistic financial plan tailored specifically for you and your situation.

A financial adviser can only do this after years of formal and ongoing training, combined with years and years of hands-on experience. Determining your financial adviser's professional qualifications will require you to ask some very pointed and maybe uncomfortable questions. You need to specifically ask exactly what professional degrees or designations they hold. In addition to their college training, you should look for professional designations like a "CFP," for Certified Financial Planner or a "CFA," for Chartered Financial Analyst. Be sure to determine that these designations are current. In order to maintain them, practitioners must meet certain continuing education requirements.

If you are going to take financial advice from people, let's make sure they have the necessary formal training, reflected in their higher educational credentials. In addition they should have ongoing, professional training, which would appear in professional designation credentials. And finally, let's make sure they have the street smarts and experience gained by doing this job successfully over a long period of time.

151

Checking References

After checking credentials, I would then ask for references. A recommendation from someone you trust and respect is actually one of the best ways to start. Ask your friends and family for recommendations of people they have heard of or have used as financial advisers. Also—if you already consult with a professional like a tax adviser or a lawyer, ask them as well. They will always have the names of a few good financial advisers who they work with and respect.

Then after you have found the names of two or three financial adviser candidates in this manner, call them and ask them for names and phone numbers of both current and former clients. Keep in mind when you make these calls that the financial adviser is not going to refer you to anyone who is going to give a negative evaluation. Because of this, you must be ready with probing questions. How satisfied are you? How long have you worked with this adviser? What is the one thing you would like to change about your adviser? You need to really be on your toes searching for what will probably be a very subtle negative hint.

Scrutinizing Fees

After checking credentials and references, you now need to ask the financial adviser how she is paid. You need to understand *exactly* how your financial adviser is getting paid. Financial advisers are typically paid in one of three ways: first by fee, where they charge a flat rate for the amount of assets under management; second, by commission, where they are paid based on what you are buying and selling within your portfolio; third, a hybrid or combination of fees and commissions.

All of these three methods work; you simply need to have your financial adviser disclose to you, up front, exactly how she is getting paid. You also have the right to know exactly how much your financial adviser is or will be compensated. If you think the compensation is out of line, all you have to do is say so. A good financial adviser will be glad to provide you with a detailed explanation.

Dr. Bob's Checklist for Hiring an Adviser

Choosing a financial adviser is probably the most important investment decision that you will ever make. No one, however, can develop a failsafe laundry list of what to look for and what to check out, because certain traits and attributes are more important to some individual investors than they are to others. In order to help you to make your final decision after you have checked your financial advisers' credentials and references and understand exactly how they are paid, here are the 10 most important questions that you should ask every financial adviser who you are thinking about working with. Let's call this list "Dr. Bob's Top 10 Questions You Should Ask of Every Financial Adviser." In true David Letterman Top 10 fashion, I am going to count these down starting with Number 10.

10. Ask them to describe their investment approach. Every financial adviser has an investment philosophy. Are they stock pickers? Quantitative black box investors or market timers? Or long-term buy and hold asset allocators?

9. Ask them what kind of reports you will receive and how often. At a minimum, you should at least receive a quarterly report. I would highly recommend a monthly report. At a minimum these reports should include the current market value of each holding in your portfolio along with performance statistics of your monthly gains and losses.

8. Ask them if they are sensitive to taxes when they do your investments. This might shock you; however, there are a lot of financial advisers who really don't care about your taxes. All they focus upon is a good investment return. I would highly recommend a financial adviser who also keeps an eye on the taxes you will have to pay. Making a lot of money on an investment idea really doesn't matter that much if you have to give most of it back in taxes.

7. Ask them specifically how their clients did in the last down market. All financial advisers appear to be the next Warren Buffett in a bull market. It is not just about making money in a bull market, but rather about protecting your assets on the downside in a bear market as well.

6. Ask them if they have ever been disciplined for unethical or improper conduct or if they have ever been sued by a client. Usually where there is smoke there will someday be fire. To me this is an important red flag to avoid.

5. Ask them what their client-to-employee ratio is. In some firms that number can actually be several thousand to one, while in other firms it is several hundred to one. There is a chance you could get lost in such a firm and may never meet the people actually making investment decisions that affect you. In other firms, the ratio may be 100 to one or even 50 to one. You need to decide how much personal care and attention you need.

4. Ask them if you become a client how easy it will be for you to fire them. This is extremely important. You need to be able to fire your financial adviser whenever you desire. You also need to make it clear that any unearned portion of any prepaid fees must be credited back to you. Never enter into a contract that obligates you to stay with and pay a financial adviser for a minimum time period.

3. Ask them what services they can offer you. Make sure that you understand everything your financial adviser and their firm has to offer. It may save you time and money to be a one-stop investment shopper.

2. Ask them specifically if they will be handling your account. You need to know exactly who you will be working with. Your initial meeting with a larger firm could actually be with a marketing and salesperson who you will never see again. I highly recommend that you be introduced to everyone on the team who will handle your money. Also, ask how often you will meet or hear from each of these people.

1. Last, but not least, ask them specifically what experience they have with working with an investor like you. If an adviser only works with high net worth clients with $5 million or more, and your assets are nowhere near that number, this financial adviser is probably not right for you. If you are a senior corporate executive, ask specifically how many other senior corporate executives they have as clients. Finally, if you have a few million dollars to invest and the average client this financial adviser works with has a few hundred thousand, again, this is probably a sign that this adviser is not right for you.

If you take only one piece of advice with you from this book, I hope it is the need to have a financial adviser to help you invest in alternative and nontraditional assets. It is never too late to start. Carl Bard said it best, "Though no one can go back and make a brand new start, anyone can start now and make a brand new ending"—especially with the assistance of a financial adviser.

ANT Valorem

- ANTs are complex investment vehicles that are best used with the help of a financial adviser.
- A financial adviser will remove the risk of investing emotionally, impulsively, and irrationally.
- A good financial adviser will tailor a financial plan specifically for you to meet your goals and dreams.
- Always be sure that you know exactly how your financial adviser is being paid.
- Make sure your financial adviser is watching the tax ramifications of your portfolio so you can keep more of what you make.

CHAPTER ELEVEN

The Axis of Evil

AVOIDING THE THREE MOST COMMON MISTAKES

Do not brood over your past mistakes and failures as this will only fill your mind with grief, regret and depression. Do not repeat them in the future.
—Swami Sivananda Saraswati,
Indian yoga master

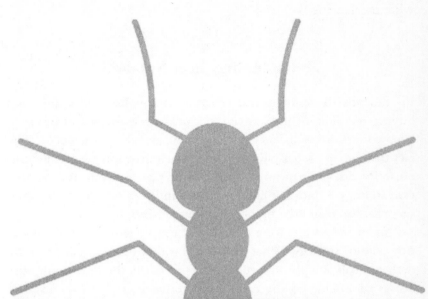

consider myself a "glass half full" kind of guy, but I think it's always a good idea to consider what *could* go wrong. When putting together an investment portfolio of alternative and non-traditional assets, this worst-case scenario is something I refer to as "The Axis of Evil."

The term "Axis of Evil" was initially used by President George W. Bush in his State of the Union Address on January 29, 2002, when he was describing the governments accused of helping terrorism; specifically, the countries that make up the axis of evil are Iraq, Iran, and North Korea. As an alternative and non-traditional asset investor, your three-part axis of evil includes:

1. Rebalancing too often
2. Revising your plan for the wrong reason
3. Attempting to do it yourself

Before we can jump into the problem of rebalancing too often let me first set the stage so you have a clear understanding of exactly what rebalancing is and isn't.

Rebalancing, in a Nutshell

In the most basic of terms, rebalancing involves the selling and buying of different investments within your portfolio in order to keep some sort of balance (or asset allocation) by asset class. The fact that you are rebalancing the individual investments within your portfolio does not mean changing your plan or your asset allocation strategy. Quite frankly by rebalancing you are actually making sure that the plan is being properly implemented.

So let me assume for a minute that everyone has an asset allocation plan or strategy. What that means is that you will have broadly defined goals and percentage targets to invest in the four major asset classes of stocks, bonds, cash, and alternative and non-traditional assets. It is important as an investor to both rebalance among these four major asset classes as well as within each of these asset classes.

What that means from an alternative and non-traditional assets perspective is that you have to determine what percentage of your investment assets need to be commodities, currencies, real estate, infrastructure, interest rate hedge, inflation hedge, derivatives, and collectibles.

Once you develop your plan, you will find that on any given day your plan is drifting from your target or goal. This happens due to the daily up and down and sideways moves in the markets. At some point some of your investments will increase while others will decrease; this will cause your portfolio to become out of balance.

Let me use commodities as an example. Let's say that your asset allocation target for commodities is 20 percent of your portfolio.

That 20 percent is divided equally among energy-based commodities 5 percent, industrial-based commodities 5 percent, precious metal–based commodities 5 percent, and agricultural-based commodities at 5 percent.

Now let's say that we have a really volatile quarter in commodities. The energy-based commodities exploded with oil and natural gas hitting an all time high. Energy-based commodities now account for 9 percent of your portfolio. Industrial-based commodities also surged, led in part by strong demand for cooper, steel, tin, and iron ore, and they now account for 7 percent of your portfolio. Precious metal commodities meanwhile entered into a bear market as both gold and silver collapsed. Now precious metals only account for 2 percent of the portfolio. Finally the demand for agriculture commodities explodes as corn, wheat, and soybeans hit a new high and agricultural commodities account for 8 percent of your portfolio.

Talk about drift. Now your portfolio has five problems. Your overall commodity exposure is now 26 percent (energy 9 percent + industrial 7 percent + precious metals 2 percent + agricultural 8 percent = 26 percent) as opposed to your target of 20 percent.

Each of the individual commodities has drifted as well. Energy-based commodities at 9 percent are 4 percent above their target of 5 percent. Industrial-based commodities at 7 percent are 2 percent above the target of 5 percent. Precious metals at 2 percent are 3 percent below the target of 5 percent. Finally agricultural commodities at 8 percent are 3 percent above the target of 5 percent.

To take care of this drift and to get things back into complete balance, here is what you need to do. Sell 4 percent of your biggest winner, energy commodities, to bring that 9 percent level back down to its target of 5 percent. Sell 2 percent of another one of your winners, industrial commodities, to bring that 7 percent back down to its target of 5 percent. Then you have to buy 3 percent of your biggest loser, precious metal commodities, to bring that

2 percent back up to its target of 5 percent. Finally you have to sell 3 percent of your second biggest winner, agricultural-based commodities, to bring that 8 percent back down to the target of 5 percent.

It is important to remember that this above rebalancing example is not reallocating your portfolio. You are really not changing anything or any strategy. All you are doing is resetting your portfolio back to your target asset allocation, no more and no less.

Buy Low and Sell High

The simplest way in the world to make money investing is to buy low and sell high. Everybody knows that. What few investors understand is that in its most basic form, rebalancing is actually creating an investment discipline that will force you to do just that, buy low and sell high. I do not mean to imply that you will always sell an asset at its absolute peak, nor does rebalancing guarantee that you will buy an asset at its absolute bottom. What rebalancing does mean is if you do it religiously enough and consistently enough in the short run, your portfolio will reap major benefits in the long run.

I don't believe that there is an investor alive today who doesn't want to buy low and sell high. Who wouldn't? You don't have to be a Wall Street guru to figure out that this is a surefire way to make money. From a theoretical perspective buying low and selling high has benefits well beyond those that first come to mind. When you sell high, you are selling your winner before it becomes a loser. That means you now have less at stake in that asset, and when it becomes a loser, you will lose less. Conversely, buying low means you are increasing your stake in a loser before it becomes a winner. That means that when it becomes a winner you are greatly increasing your eventual gains.

The Axis of Evil

Reversion to the Mean

Let me make this really simple for you. I can explain exactly why rebalancing works. It's called "reversion to the mean," a well-known mathematical and statistical phenomenon. What this statistical phenomenon has proved is that things can't stay far above or far below their long-term average for very long. At some point the hot streak or the cold streak comes to an end. From an investment perspective that means the long-term average remains intact. This is true of every NFL quarterback who has had a run of 300-plus-yards passing days as well as the NFL running back who has had back-to-back 200-yard running days. At some point reversion of the mean kicks in. Its true in NFL football, and it is true in investing as well.

The Contrarian

I have had the pleasure in my career to work with and become personal friends with the greatest contrarian investor of all time, David Dreman of Dreman Value Advisors. I bring up this point now because in some ways rebalancing is a lot like being a contrarian investor. The reason is because rebalancing is counterintuitive. When you rebalance, you are a contrarian because you are doing just the opposite of what the financial media is telling everyone to do. When you rebalance you are selling out of your hottest and best investments. Even worse than that, you are now buying into the investments that are dead cold, the ones that are losing you the most money. Most investors are not able to do that. It is not easy to become a contrarian investor.

Let me tell you from firsthand experience the pressures a contrarian investor faces every day. As you rebalance and sell your winners so you can buy your losers, your gut is telling you that you are wrong. The reason is that the financial media is bombarding you with reasons why the investment you just sold is the best investment ever, while the investment you just bought is the single worst investment of all time.

163

Just the Facts

No matter what your gut tells you or the media tells you about rebalancing, it is important to remember these three facts:

1. Rebalancing is a scientific, time-tested investment strategy that will get you better returns while reducing your risks.
2. Rebalancing doesn't rely on a crystal ball. You don't need some hot tip or inside scoop to do your rebalancing. In this day and age, there is no such thing as a hot tip. By the time something is reported on CNBC or written about in the *Wall Street Journal* it is already too late to act on it. Here is my golden rule, and you can take this one to the bank. If it's in the news it's already in the price.
3. The most sophisticated institutional money managers do it. If they rebalance why shouldn't you?

Axis #1: Rebalancing Too Often

So here is the classic rebalancing problem. If you do it too often, you will sell your best assets too early before they peak. Also you will find yourself investing in falling assets way too early, clearly before they bottom. On the other side of the coin, if you rebalance too seldom, you will ride your winners way too long past their peak, where they will then be losers. You will also run the risk of letting your portfolio drift away from the intended asset allocation strategy.

Strategy #1: Fixed Date

One strategy is to rebalance on a fixed date; once a year is a popular choice. This annual rebalancing is the single most popular choice, because it is not overly burdensome and it is easy to remember.

While this may be the easiest answer it is not the best answer. Rebalancing only once a year isn't often enough to take advantage of market changes. For the average, at the very least, investors should rebalance three times a year or every four months.

Strategy #2: Fixed Opportunity

The best rebalancing schedule is the one that you cannot set in advance. The schedule is triggered by your portfolio itself. If it drifts too far, then you need to rebalance. Only you can determine how far is too far. Some major institutional investors are comfortable if the range is +/−20 percent, while some retail investors are concerned if it is +/− 2 percent.

Axis #2: Revising Your Plan for the Wrong Reason

So now that we have a plan, let me ask you a basic question. Why would we change it? The answer is simple, because things change.

Some of the changes are gradual and expected, like aging. Others can be unexpected, like job changes or divorce. Whatever the cause, that is the perfect reason to look at your asset allocation plan.

This is *very* important. I am not talking about market timing here. The changes that should drive you to change your asset allocation have nothing to do with the state of the markets themselves. Rather they are changes to your lifestyle.

Let's look at both of these major categories: expected gradual life changes and unexpected sudden life changes.

Category #1: Expected Gradual Changes

The single most important gradual change that will affect all of us is the simple fact of life that we are all going to age. Aging is not just a physical process; aging will also have ramifications on your investment asset allocation plan.

When you age, your lifestyle changes, as does your investment time horizon. A 40-year-old has a lot more time to recover and recoup from investment hiccups than an 80-year-old does.

As we age, the chances of our health deteriorating greatly increases as does the likelihood that we will be spending more and more on health care, health care services, and medications. In the United States, from the time of birth until children celebrate their fifth birthday, parents give their children on average eight different prescription drugs a year. Meanwhile, watch what happens when we age. The average 75-year-old in the United States currently uses 18 different prescription drugs a year. That trend helps explain why with only 5 percent of the world's population the United States accounts for over 40 percent of the world's pharmaceutical sales. With this backdrop it is important to now be invested in very liquid assets, so you can get to your money at a moment's notice.

Category #2: Unexpected Sudden Changes

Some things in life happen rather fast, and we don't really see them coming until all of a sudden they are here. I call these "life-changing" events. When you have a life-changing event, you should also make sure that the event is reflected in changes made to your asset allocation plan as well. These unexpected changes can be both good and bad. It could be the result of a marriage or the result of a divorce. It could be the happy time of celebrating a birth or the sad time of mourning a death. Here is a simple rule of thumb: Whenever you have a life-changing event, think about what that means to your asset allocation strategy.

One other unexpected and sudden change that is bound to happen sometime in your life revolves around your job. You may get a big promotion, or a big bonus, or get fired, or get laid off, or your company goes bankrupt, or your company gets bought, and you are given a boatload of stock. In some way, shape, or form, your job is someday going to unexpectedly change your life. When it does, make sure you change your asset allocation as well.

Axis #3: Bill, Don't Be a Hero

Let me bring this chapter to a close by briefly focusing on the third and the biggest mistake an investor can make, and that is attempting to do it yourself. Even though I devoted the entire last chapter to how and why you need a financial adviser, this chapter on rebalancing may really show you why you should never try to rebalance without a financial adviser. While on the surface you may think, *How hard can this rebalance thing be? All I have is stocks, bonds, cash and alternative investments.* Well, let's take a quick peek under the hood, and you will quickly see just how complicated it actually is.

Challenge #1: Stocks Rebalance

So you really want to rebalance your stock portfolio on your own? Good luck. How much are you going to put in large-capitalization stocks versus mid-capitalization stocks versus small-capitalization stocks versus micro-capitalization stocks? And what about styles of investing? How much in value versus growth versus blend? Are you going to buy any preferred stock as well?

Where are your stock investments going to be? Canada, EAFE countries (Europe, Australasia, and the Far East), or just Europe? How about developed Asia and Japan? Don't forget the United Kingdom, or how about Asia ex-Japan? Emerging Europe, like Poland, is an option as is the Middle East and Africa. Or Latin America or maybe the frontier markets like Vietnam. Hopefully, you get my point.

Challenge #2: Bonds Rebalance

It's just as bad or complicated for an asset class that on the surface seems simple, like bonds. So exactly what kind of bonds do you rebalance to, U.S. Treasury bonds, agency bonds, corporate bonds? Don't forget high-yield corporate bonds. Maybe you would rather have municipal bonds or asset-backed bonds or guaranteed investment contracts. How about a few credit default swaps?

Again, where are your bond investments going to be? Canada, EAFE countries (Europe, Australasia, and the Far East), or just Europe? How about Developed Asia and Japan. Don't forget the United Kingdom, or how about Asia ex-Japan? Emerging Europe like Poland is an option as is the Middle East and Africa. Or Latin America or maybe the frontier markets like Vietnam. Am I making my point?

Challenge #3: Cash Rebalance

Even simple things like cash investments are not so simple. Do you want the physical cash? How about a money market fund or maybe a certificate of deposit? Or a bankers acceptance note or a repurchase agreement?

Challenge #4: Alternative and Non-Traditional Rebalance

Finally the most complicated of all rebalancing is in the alternative and non-traditional assets. So let's start with commodities. Do you want to take physical possession? What type of commodities? Energy-based commodities like oil and natural gas; industrial-based commodities like copper, steel, tin, and iron ore; precious metals like gold or silver? Don't forget the agricultural-based commodities of corn, wheat, soybean, cattle, and livestock.

What about currencies? Again, where will your currency investments be? Canada, EAFE countries (Europe, Australasia, and the Far East), or just Europe? How about Developed Asia and Japan? Don't forget the United Kingdom, or how about Asia ex-Japan? Emerging Europe, like Poland, is an option as is the Middle East and Africa, or Latin America or maybe the frontier markets like Vietnam.

Moving on to real estate, will you be rebalancing into apartments, commercial, industrial, residential, office, farmlands, real estate investment trusts, hotels? And where are you getting that real estate exposure? Will it all be in the United States, or will you be in countries like Canada, EAFE countries (Europe, Australasia, and the Far East), or just Europe? How about developed Asia and Japan? Don't forget the United Kingdom, or how about Asia ex-Japan? Emerging Europe, like Poland, is an option as is the Middle East and Africa, or Latin America or maybe the frontier markets like Vietnam?

I think you get my point, and I haven't even touched upon the other major alternative and non-traditional asset classes of infrastructure, interest rate hedges, inflation hedges, derivatives including futures and forwards and options and swaps, and finally, collectibles like art and rare coins and stamps and classic cars and wine.

I have said this before, and I will say it again; maybe the single most important investment decision you will ever make is hiring a financial adviser. Think of it this way: If you really want to, you could manufacture or make your own computer. Because they make millions of them, Dell has gotten pretty good at it. They now can make high quality computers for as little as a few hundred dollars. Just think about what it would cost you to build your own computer. You might be able to do it, but it would take a huge commitment of time and money to learn the science, purchase the materials, and then execute the necessary procedures. I am sure your finished product would be shabby in comparison.

Investment decision making should be looked at the same way. You can make investment decisions or take the advice of an experienced professional. The investment decisions of individuals are commonly costly and mediocre. Why? Because the investment world is filled with foreign concepts, esoteric language, legal rules, and a vast array of methodologies.

Orson Welles once said, "We're born ALONE, we live ALONE and we die ALONE." Note that he didn't say we should invest ALONE and neither have I!

ANT Valorem

- Rebalancing does not mean you are changing your asset allocation strategy.
- Rebalancing creates an investment discipline that will force you to buy low and sell high.
- As you get older, your time horizons change; so should your investment strategy.
- With every life-changing event, you should revisit your asset allocation strategy.
- The single most important investment decision you will ever make is hiring a financial adviser.

CHAPTER TWELVE

ANT Attack

DEVELOPING YOUR ANTs PORTFOLIO

Diversification is a protection against ignorance.
—Warren Buffett

Now it is time to put everything together and make some money. Hopefully this chapter will help you do just that by using it as a guide when you sit down with your financial adviser. Together the two of you can customize a plan just for you to help you reach your financial goals while keeping in mind your risk tolerances.

Rethinking Your Asset Allocation

Let me begin with a basic and very general asset allocation recommendation. I am going to keep this simple and just use the broadest of categories: stocks, bonds, cash, and alternatives or ANTs. The general consensus on Wall Street today is an asset allocation of 45 percent in stocks, 30 percent in bonds, 15 percent in alternatives, and 10 percent in cash.

I have a different view of the world where I recommend 60 percent in stocks, only 5 percent in bonds, 30 percent in alternatives, and only 5 percent in cash. In terms of where I stand versus the consensus view on Wall Street, I am recommending investors overweight stocks, underweight bonds, overweight alternatives, and underweight cash. My single biggest overweight is in the area of alternatives, where I think investors should have at least 30 percent of their portfolio.

> *My single biggest overweight is in the area of alternatives, where I think investors should have at least 30 percent of their portfolio.*

Developing Your ANTs Portfolio

In developing my ANTs portfolio I want to make sure that I am diversified over a broad range of alternative investment strategies and options.

Dr. Bob's ANTs Portfolio

30% Commodities
My single biggest exposure would be in commodities, which in my view are the best long-term opportunity of all. I would divide my 30% exposure up as follows:

  10% Copper: iPath Dow Jones UBS Subindex Total Return
  10% Gold: SPDR Gold Trust
  10% Corn: ETES Corn ETF

15% Inflation Hedge
My second largest exposure would be an inflation hedge. I would put all 15 percent in iShare Barclays TIPS Bond Fund.

15% Interest Rate Hedge
Also at 15 percent would be my interest rate hedge. I recommend the entire 15 percent go into a Senior Secured Floating Rate Fund from Hartford called Hartford Floating Rate Fund (HFLAX).

15% Infrastructure
I would also place 15 percent in infrastructure. I would divide my 15 percent exposure up three ways:

    5% Sterling Construction Company (STRL.O)
    5% Fraport AG (FA)
    5% Emerging Global Share China Infrastructure (CHXX)

10% Derivatives
I would put 10 percent into derivatives, and both would be in a long call position. I would split the 10 percent up as follows:

    5% long call on C.M.E. Group (CME)
    5% long call on Pro Share Ultra Short 20+ Year Treasury
        ETF (TBT)

5% Real Estate
I want my real estate exposure to be global so I would put the entire 5 percent in an Asia REIT, iShare FTSE EPRA/NAREIT Asia Index ETF (IFAS).

5% Currency
I would put 5 percent in currency by shorting the euro-dollar. As Europe slips into a double dip recession at the same time the United States begins to raise interest rates the dollar will rise as the euro drops.

5% Collectibles
My final 5 percent goes into collectibles. I would put the entire 5 percent into wine by investing in the Vintage Fund.

This portfolio should provide you and your adviser with a great starting point to make sure that your portfolio is exposed to my ANTs investment strategy.

In Closing

Let me bring this book to a close with one of the most famous Chinese proverbs: "If you are planning for a year, sow rice; if you are planning for a decade, plant trees; if you are planning for a lifetime, educate people."

It is my hope that the preceding pages have helped to educate you about ANTs.

 ANT Valorem

- Make sure your investment portfolio has an overweight in alternative investments, ANTs.
- Stay broadly diversified across a broad spectrum of alternative investments.
- Always work with a professional financial adviser.
- Dr. Bob's ANTs Portfolio:
  - 30% Commodities
  - 15% Inflation hedge
  - 15% Interest rate hedge
  - 15% Infrastructure
  - 10% Derivatives
  - 5% Real estate
  - 5% Currency
  - 5% Collectibles

ANTSpeak

A UNIQUE GLOSSARY OF ALTERNATIVE AND NON-TRADITIONAL INVESTMENT TERMS (OPINIONS INCLUDED)

I am very much afraid of definitions, and yet one is almost forced to make them. One must take care, too, not to be inhibited by them.

—Robert Delaunay, French artist